Pet-tecture

Pet-tecture
Design for Pets

Tom Wainwright

Contemporary Design for Pets

Pet-tecture: Design for Pets explores the fascinating world of architecture for animals. More specifically, it is a collection of homes and play areas for pets, conceived and crafted by some of the leading architects and designers from around the globe – works that are characterised not only by their pleasing aesthetic, but also for the ingenuity of their designs and, perhaps above all, for their intrinsic reminder of just how lucky we are as humans to live alongside the diverse domesticated creatures for whom they are intended.

It is all too easy in this day and age to take pets for granted. We are so used to the idea of dogs and cats being a part of our families that we rarely stop and look at these creatures that live alongside us for what they used to be: wild animals. One important step in the animal-to-pet evolution was the development of the working relationship impinged on animals by humans. Fossils, carvings, and cave paintings suggest that dogs, for example, would have been domesticized as early as two and a half million years ago during the Palaeolithic period. They provided, through selective breeding, crucial support for essential activities such as hunting, herding, safe-guarding the home, and even competing in sports, all in return for shelter, food, and companionship. This arrangement

can be described as a symbiotic relationship: a mutually beneficial concord that brings pleasure to the owner, and is seemingly similarly appreciated by the animal.

Historically this essentially practical relationship has sometimes been taken to another level altogether. Our feline friends, for example, were highly prized in Ancient Egypt for their ability to catch vermin and even kill dangerous snakes. These qualities, in combination with its inherently graceful poise, elevated it to god-like status – in the form of the half-cat-half-woman goddess Bastet. Cats may no longer be worshipped but they are certainly often adored by their human companions. Moreover, such relationships that go beyond the purely practical also point to another form of bond between humans and pets: one of companionship, but founded substantially on aesthetics. An example of this would include the Chihuahua: prized for its petite size and cute appearance it is also, for some, the perfect 'handbag dog'.

Thus far only cats and dogs have been mentioned, but what other animals or, indeed, birds or fish or insects count as human pets? Traditionally, pets have been restricted to those creatures that are housed – whether in aquaria, aviary, bowl, cage, hive, hutch, kennel, paddock, or stable – within, or in very close proximity to, a human household. However, the increasing popularity during the latter years of the twentieth century, of 'petting zoos', which encourage children, especially those brought up in urban environments, to see and touch farm, and even some wild animals, has effectively extended the definition. As we shall see, even kangaroos count now, and of course one important consequence of this is architectural: the types of structures that now come under the umbrella of Pet-tecture are significantly more numerous than they once were.

Of course, the whole concept of 'pet architecture' is a relatively recent phenomenon too. In fact, it has only been in the twenty-first century that architectural designs for pets have gradually begun to acquire not dissimilar status to human architecture. In much the same way that, certainly for the last two to three hundred years, just about every eminent building designer – from Robert Adam in the eighteenth century, to Le Corbusier in the twentieth, to Zaha Hadid in the twenty-first – has at least at one point in his or her career turned their attention to designing a chair, so award-winning architects of the here-and-now are increasingly keen to include Pet-tecture in their portfolio.

In addition to winning awards, peer-group kudos and pet-owner admiration, there are also, not surprisingly, commercial reasons for this development. For example, in the United States alone the 'pet ownership' industry is a multi-million dollar business. In 2016, it was estimated that people in the United States spent an estimated $66.75 billion per annum on pets, with a similar amount, proportionate to the population, in the United Kingdom. Granted, food and veterinary bills account for a high percentage of this, but the spend on the rest, including accommodation, play areas and accessories is still huge and, according to market research, growing ever bigger.

On a personal note, my own excitement at this burgeoning of design for pets is, to a considerable degree, shaped by some of my strongest memories from childhood. Growing up, our family pet was Digby, then commonly known as a 'Spandoodle' – a cross between a Spaniel and a Poodle, and nowadays better-known as a 'Cockapoo'. Digby didn't have a kennel as such, although he wasn't averse to kennelling himself under our dining room table if he didn't fancy going out for a walk in the rain. However, over the years he had numerous beds, comprised of cast-off bean bags. I've no doubt Digby really appreciated all of them – aside from sleeping, they were the go-to place for chewing, whether given bones or stolen shoes or gloves. They were not only human cast-offs, they were also, despite being undoubtedly practical, something of a decorative eyesore and as far from being 'en-suite' with the interior design and furnishing of our home as one could get.

So I was delighted when I began to discover, well over a decade later, the extent to which the good old bean-bag has been superseded by amazingly innovative architect, interior designer, and artist-generated designs fashioned from materials as diverse as steel, plywood, artificial turf, felt and concrete (to name but a few), and constructed to standards equivalent to, and sometimes exceeding, those for human architecture and furnishings.

In the following pages you will discover over two hundred examples of these modern designs for pets. All are underpinned by a simple but admirable goal: to care and provide for our pets. However, as you will see, the sheer diversity of the designs and the materials used means no two are alike and, ergo, just about all tastes – human and animal – are catered for. For example, on the one hand Abramson Teiger Architects' *Cat in the Fishbowl* shelter (p.217) would not look out of place as a model for a modern civic or residential complex. Conversely, Perkins+Will's *UnFURled* (p.245), also for cats, adopts a more recreational approach with its rollercoaster-like loops and ribbon-like twirls.

Whether practical or playful, many of the projects featured are also characterized by an adventurous use of repurposed items and scrap materials. One such construction is Shigeru Ban's *Papier Papillon* (p.136), a structure for dogs made from

cardboard tubes originally employed, amongst other uses, as the centre rolls of bubble wrap. Similarly, the Welsh company JAM Furniture fashioned their *Nestbox* roost for birds (p.235) from metal sheets salvaged from old washing machines and dishwashers, together with wooden off-cuts obtained from local businesses. Likewise, d3architeture assembled their *Alley Cats: HVAC edition* (p.81) from a discarded air conditioning unit – a particularly appropriate source of materials as the construction was primarily intended as an outdoor shelter for feral cats, who are very accustomed to sheltering in human discards found out on the street.

In a world that produces an enormous amount of un-recyclable plastic, it is particularly great to discover just how many designers have incorporated recycled or sustainably sourced materials into their designs. Indeed, Formation Association even goes so far as to incorporate low-maintenance plants into their *Flora-Gato* (p.163), a shelter-cum-seating area that is dotted with vibrant Spanish Moss and Korean Grass. Materials such as the cedar wood used in Matthew Hayward and Nadia Turan's modern chicken coop *The Nogg* (p.104) is not only sustainably sourced, but in this particular instance, ideal for housing animals as the wood is naturally resistant to bacterial growth. Eco-friendly designs are much in evidence, but only if they are suitable for pets. For example, the *NekoHut* by Blink Pet (p.147) was made from wicker-work because the designer's own cat has a pronounced liking for natural fibres, with straw being a particular favourite. More generally, sisal fibre, when fashioned into rope, is perfect for all cats: durable and particularly resistant to sharp claws, it was the ideal material for designer Erik Stehmann's *DOG Scratchpost for Cats* (p.177), which is hand-clad in sisal rope. The durability of the material is, of course, just as important when it comes to outdoor use and resistance to the weather. Thus, Filippo Pisan's bird house *Nest N°1* (p.140) has a Cor-Ten steel roof – its orange, rust-like surface proving that the practical can also be beautiful. Conversely, the beautiful can be practical, and fun too: New York-based designer Hugh Hayden's *HEX Tennis Dog Bed* (p.220), is a particularly good example of this. Made entirely from tennis balls, it's a fusion of a sleeping area and most canine's favourite toy – a dog's dream.

The sleep-and-play combination, and in some cases incorporating things for eating, is evident in many of the designs. Multi-purpose examples include the *Built-in Dog Bed* at the Lin Residence (p.190), by architecture and interior design firm LCGA Design: a side-table, a dog bed and a display shelf all-in-one, it can also serve in an open-plan space as a room-divider. Equally, the *Cat-à-Tête* by Formation Association (p.89) is a cat shelter and human seating rolled into one, its S-shaped configuration encouraging

humans and cats to sit and interact with one another. Interaction is also evident, albeit on a more overtly educational level, in Francesco Faccin's *Honey Factory* (p.110), which not only boards bees, but also emboldens people to view the bees through a large glass door, thereby enabling them, through familiarity, to gradually lose any inherent fear of the insects.

The aforementioned three projects highlight a particularly important aspect of Pet-tecture: some of the more interesting designs are usually those that work well for not only the animal, but also the human – both ergonomically and, certainly in the case of the human, aesthetically too. For example, the designer's awareness of space and practicality is clearly evident in Seungji Mun's *Dog House Sofa* (p.92), which took a standard double-seated sofa and incorporated a wooden dog den under the arm, thus saving interior space while bringing the pet into the folds of everyday family life. In the same vein, the *Catissa Cat House* (p.148) reduces floor clutter with its wall-mounted modular design, all the while providing exciting climbing opportunities for its feline occupants. This multi-functionality can also be seen in LYCS Architecture's modular *CATable 2.0* (p.46), which can be employed as a stool, a table and a bookshelf.

The specific inspiration for many of the Pet-tecture designs varies considerably. However, a number of them were fuelled by pet owners simply being unable to find suitable existing designs that catered for both theirs and their pet's needs, and who therefore adopted an 'if you want something done right, you have to do it yourself' attitude, and set about making it themselves. I was particularly moved by architect Hiroshi Naito's account of creating his *Dog Cooler* (p.200). Without air-conditioning, Hiroshi's faithful, fluffy-haired dog, Pepe the Spitz, would get extremely hot during the Japanese summers. He would cool himself by lying on the ceramic-tiled floor of the bathroom, but would still pant as if in some discomfort. When Pepe passed away, at the ripe old age of 16, Hiroshi, by way of tribute to his deceased companion, designed the ingenious cooler, comprising a framework of aluminium tubing and wooden slats into which cooling bags of ice could be inserted.

Several other projects have charitable origins. Notable examples include those conceived for the annual Giving Shelter event: an Architects for Animals awareness-raising initiative in support of FixNation, a non-profit organisation that offers a free-of-charge spay and neuter service for feral cats in the San Fernando Valley area of Los Angeles. Some of the feral cat shelters that have emerged from this are among the most innovative projects in the book. For example, Standard Architecture's *Catosphere* (p.105), is an amazing spaceship-like

structure that can regulate internal temperature via its moveable louvered wood walls, while Abramson Teiger Architect's *Ball of Twine* (p.102) imaginatively plays with function and proportion by transforming a classic cat plaything, a ball of string, into something it can also sleep in.

Even more peculiar designs are to be found in Artist Aki Inomata's shelters for hermit crabs (p.122), which were inspired by the 'No Mans Land' exhibition at the French Embassy in Japan in 2009. The exhibition was in response to the French returning some of their embassy land to Japanese ownership – a peaceful exchange and one that would be returned to the French after fifty years. The manner in which the status of this land had been redefined reminded Aki Inomata of how hermit crabs often change their shells – the exterior changing, but not the crab inside. The result was her 3D-printed resin shelters for hermit crabs, configured as iconic landmark buildings from around the world. When the crabs moved between the buildings it looked as if they were 'crossing over national borders', thereby bringing to mind what it must be like for refugees and migrants having to cross borders and even change nationalities when fleeing their homes.

Symbolically, the role of the artists and designers in Pet-tecture can certainly run deep. Leopold Banchini and Daniel Zamarbide's *Parole* cage (p.124) was modelled on the Champ-Dollon prison in Switzerland – known for housing almost twice as many inmates as its capacity. Their scaled-down structure is designed for laboratory mice, and although it was built to question the moral role of the architect when designing institutions such as prisons, it also makes us fundamentally question how we treat animals. Is a cage an acceptable design to house animals in? And what does caging an animal say about human-animal relationships?

Also in that vein, architect Sou Fujimoto wanted to rebalance the pet-owner relationship by bringing the family dog into the everyday goings-on of family life. His *No Dog, No Life!* (p.63), provides a designated space for a dog surrounded by shelves that house both pet and human items. This type of animal-conscious, sensitive design is by no means confined to mice, cats and dogs. The Cornwall-based Green&Blue studio, for example, have created a number of designs for bees and wild birds, in an impassioned attempt to protect the environment for future generations. With the declining bee population in mind, their *Bee Block & Bee Brick* (p.171) are particularly stylish attempts to provide nesting spaces for solitary bees – spaces that are increasingly hard to find.

The spirit underpinning this animal-conscious approach to design is especially evident in the Architecture for Dogs collection – a design initiative from the Hara Design Institute and the Nippon Design Centre, under the direction of renowned designer Kenya Hara, who gathered together thirteen of the best architects and designers in Japan to design structures specifically for dogs that could be made by anyone following online blueprints and tutorials. A specific breed of dog inspired each design. Thus, for example, a Jack Russell who found contentment in nestling in its owner's clothes inspired the creation of Torafu Architect's *Wanmock* (p.16), which inventively incorporates old t-shirts or jumpers into the centre of the structure. Perhaps above all, each of the thirteen Architecture for Dogs designs is a recognition of just how much our pets mean to us – and that lies right at the heart of what this book, *Pet-tecture: Design for Pets*, is really meant to be: a practical, aesthetic and symbolic celebration of animal-human companionship through design.

Notes

Pet-tecture includes a number of special features, as follows: at the top of each project is the name of the design, followed by the name of the designer, artist, architect, manufacturer or company who created the design.

Under this are the pet icons that identify which animal, or animals, the design was intended for. Next to the pet icon(s), material icons show the primary materials used in the construction of each design.

At the bottom of each page can be found animal track marks that represent the relevant pet's footprints.

The full range of icons can be found opposite.

Key to Footprints

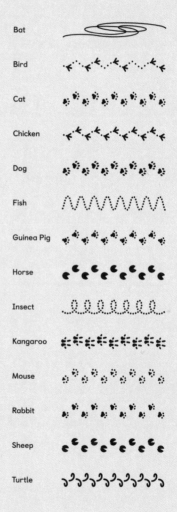

Bat	
Bird	
Cat	
Chicken	
Dog	
Fish	
Guinea Pig	
Horse	
Insect	
Kangaroo	
Mouse	
Rabbit	
Sheep	
Turtle	

Key to Pets

Bat   Bird   Cat   Chicken   Dog

Fish   Guinea Pig   Horse   Insect   Kangaroo

Mouse   Rabbit   Sheep   Turtle

Key to Materials

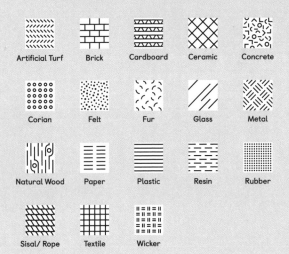

Artificial Turf   Brick   Cardboard   Ceramic   Concrete

Corian   Felt   Fur   Glass   Metal

Natural Wood   Paper   Plastic   Resin   Rubber

Sisal/ Rope   Textile   Wicker

"Until one has loved
an animal, a part of one's soul
remains unawakened."

Anatole France

Name of Design:
Wanmock
Name of Company:
Torafu Architects

For Kenya Hara and the Nippon Design Centre's Architecture for Dogs initiative, Japanese firm Torafu Architects created this design for the Jack Russell. The designers discovered that the excitable and loyal terriers find great comfort in the smell and fabric of their owner's clothes. The resulting design allows for a T-shirt or jumper to be stretched across a plywood frame to create a hammock for the dog. The name of the design perfectly fits the product: 'wan' is the Japanese equivalent of 'woof', and 'mock' refers to the hammock design. The easy DIY frame's blueprints are available on the Architecture for Dogs website.

Unable to find well-made and distinctive furniture for pets and people alike, friends Marc Ange and Frédéric Stouls have dedicated themselves to 'creating the extraordinary' via Ange's creative studio Bloom Room. Manufactured in France and Italy by luxury pet brand Chimère, this Mid-Century Modern-inspired sofa for cats and dogs is available in two different sizes. Completely handmade, the sofa comprises a solid oak base with aluminium legs running under it. The sofa's frame and cushion are upholstered in Kvadrat fabric in typically chic colours, and bespoke finishes are also available on request.

Name of Design:
The Bed
Name of Company:
Meyou Paris

Reminiscent of a protective cover over a pram, this cosy bed for cats is an ideal place to snuggle up and get warm. Standing 63.5 centimeters (25 inches) off the ground, the Bed provides the perfect place for the sneakiest cats to keep their surroundings under surveillance. The engulfing hood is made of one hundred per cent pure wool felt – a popular material for cats – under which a polyester cushion is supported by a four-legged platform made of sturdy and sleek solid beech wood. Meyou Paris specializes in creating beautiful products that respect the needs of a well-designed home, but with a cat's comfort in mind.

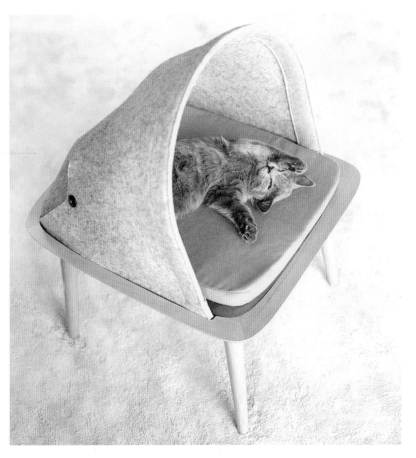

This chic bird feeder oozes simplicity and style. The egg-shaped feeder is handcrafted in stoneware and finished in a variety of glossy colours. Weighing just less than a kilo (two pounds), the egg is suspended by a vinyl-coated wire and relies on gravity to keep it stable for visiting birds. Two overlapping aluminium poles puncture the bottom of the egg, creating four perches from which birds can feed. Birdfood is placed inside the egg, filling up the custom-spun aluminium dish that contains four small drainage holes. The egg is easily refilled, simply by turning it upside down and removing the base and poles.

Name of Design:
Birdhouse
Name of Company:
Studio PAULBAUT

From Studio PAULBAUT comes this beautiful design that was formed using laser-cut birch plywood. Based on the method of construction used for the Rocking-2-Gether Chair (p.207) by the same designer, the Birdhouse is constructed by forming the 3D models digitally. Several prototypes were 3D-printed to test and develop the design, the wood is laser cut into shape to make the final product. Aluminium spacers sit on six millimetre ($\frac{1}{4}$ inch) metal rods that distance the ribs. The 'burnt' aesthetic effect comes from the laser cut wood, with a clear finish coating applied to protect it from weathering.

Glenn Ross established Vurv Design in British Columbia, Canada in 2001, and remains its principal designer and maker, using his craftsmanship to fashion truly unique designs. With a 'function first' attitude towards his work, this modern and delightful piece is comfortable as well as stylish. The bent plywood is curved into a large 'C' that draws focus to the resting area, which hides a luxuriously fluffy fur bed. Supporting the pod are two wood veneer legs that curve away from the floor, giving the pooch pride of place. This versatile style calls to mind a classic Mid-Century Modern aesthetic that would suit any home.

Name of Design:
Casa Lapiz
Name of Company:
Productora

Originally conceived as a practical sculpture as part of the *Dogchitecture* exhibition in Mexico, the pyramidal form of the Casa Lapiz (or Pencil House) helps protect dogs from rain or harsh sunlight, while adding a touch of drama to the garden as a piece of art in its own right. A small triangular opening at the peak of one of the four sides acts as a vent, and a large triangular opening on another side forms an entrance that is large enough for a medium-sized dog. Crafted from MDF board, the structure is painted in water-resistant polyester, making the Casa Lapiz weatherproof, bright and durable.

Name of Design:
Bubble Bed
Name of Company:
B.pet

In true Italian style, this dog bed by Italian brand B.pet is perfect for the most fashion-conscious pets. With hints of iconic 1960s furniture design, the original Bubble Beds featured a Plexiglass frame, thermo-shaped by hand, resting on a chromium base plate. A high-quality, fabric cushion of a cotton-and-viscose blend adorns the seat for the dog's comfort. The limited edition pictured here, however, is luxuriously plated with 24-carat gold. An eiderdown-stuffed, 100 per cent silk cushion provides the final lavish touch, making this bed one of the most decadent canine designs – perfect for man's best friend.

Name of Design:
Geometric Cat Bed
Name of Company:
LikeKittysVille

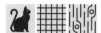

Handmade by designer Jayne Blume in Texas, these geometric, wall-mounted 'cat shelves' are ideal for curious cats to spy on their surroundings, as well as providing an elevated napping spot. The simple structure is fixed to the wall with two screws and comprises a frame made of sustainably grown plywood, held together by glue. The top surface of the bed juts diagonally upwards creating a protective, cosy area for cats to cradle in, as well as giving the design its distinctive look. Encasing the bed is a removable, machine-washable slipcover made from recycled, vintage fabrics.

Name of Design:
Retro Dog Bed
Name of Company:
Bohemian Workbench

Based in Venice, California, Charles Lushear is renowned for his use of premium materials and entirely handcrafted designs, produced by his studio Bohemian Workbench. The resulting products are distinctive conversation pieces, blending the notions of modern technology with natural wood and retro aesthetics. This dog bed calls to mind the silhouette of the friendly robot Stars Wars character R2D2, but is predominantly made of walnut. The enclosed, cosy structure features a sloping roof with mahogany and ebony design accents, as well as a rectangular cushion with vintage-style fabric.

Name of Design:
Cat Canopy Lounge
Name of Company:
CANOPYstudio

Reminiscent of the smaller element of the iconic Lounge Chair and Ottoman designed by Charles and Ray Eames in 1956, this handcrafted, feline podium was conceived by Kat Webster, of Louisiana-based CANOPYstudio. Like its Eames predecessor, the Canopy Lounge has an elegant, streamlined form characteristic of the Mid-Century Modern aesthetic. The rich, walnut-veneered, bent-plywood shell supports a brightly coloured cushion that is secured in place with magnets embedded in the wood. Available in various colours, the cushions would certainly complement any interior, or indeed, cat.

Name of Design:
D&C House
Name of Designer:
Julia Kononenko

Combining the functions of a bedside table with a pet bed, the D&C House by Ukrainian designer Julia Kononenko is the perfect place for your pet to snuggle up next to you at bedtime – without hogging the whole bed. Constructed from wood, the house is bolstered by eight asymmetrical legs, and has the option of being painted black or white, or left with a natural wood finish. The five-sided opening is large enough for a cat or small dog, and a snug rectangular cushion forms the base of the bed. A handy cupboard on the side is perfect for grooming products, but could also hide your pet's most prized toys or treats.

Name of Design:
Landmarks
Name of Company:
Poopy Cat

If cats ruled the world (which they might already do), they would most certainly choose to reside in prestigious and symbolically powerful abodes. Made solely from cardboard, delivered flat-packed and easy to assemble, these cat dens are inspired by historic architectural wonders. The design to the right, for example, recalls St Basil's Cathedral in Moscow, while the zoomorphic house below is modelled on the Great Sphinx of Giza – particularly appropriate, given cats were worshipped as gods in ancient Egypt. For the more presidential feline, a White House inspired design is also available.

"Thousands of years ago, cats were worshipped as gods. Cats have never forgotten this."

Anonymous

Name of Design:
Cage Archibird
Name of Company:
Grégoire de Laforrest

Calling to mind a Cabinet of Curiosities, this bird home falls halfway between practical furniture and showstopping sculpture. The purity of the materials brings the viewer closer to nature: the natural finish of the solid oak table is pefectly complemented by the model of a tree, which also functions as a familiar perch for the birds. The uppermost branches of the white-lacqured tree rise through the table, allowing the birds to better view their surroundings through three glass bell domes. Supported by four legs, the oak base of the birdcage connects to the bottom of the table with stainless steel cables.

Name of Design:
CATCUBE
Name of Company:
Standard
Architecture

The Architects for Animals Giving Shelter fundraiser in 2014 saw top Los Angeles-based architects design and create cat houses for an exhibition and charity event at FixNation – a non-profit organization committed to neutering and spaying feral cats. Made of concrete and reclaimed wood, the sixty centimetre square (two square foot) cube is designed to retain heat throughout the day, keeping the interior warm during cold nights. Inside, the shelter is divided by a piece of timber and the garage-like front wall can be fully opened up or closed down, as the cats prefer.

This delightful, polygonal dog house was created by Bad Marlon Design Studio, based in South Korea. The main purpose of this design was to incorporate natural light into the house, via charming triangular punched holes along the walls and ceiling that trace the sun's movement throughout the day. Wanting to create an environment of same-design-identity between dog and owner, the aim is for pets to enjoy the sunrise and sunset just as humans do. Made from powder-coated steel, the white exterior adds to the aesthetic lightness of the structure, making it perfectly suitable for modern or contemporary interiors.

Name of Design:
The Pet Project
Name of Company:
**Marie Laurent
Architecture**

This award-winning pet bed caters for both cats and dogs. Appropriate for indoor and outdoor use, this gable-roofed home comes on wheels, making it practical and easily portable. The project came from the desire to give pets their own designated space, something that can be forgotten when designing a home. The roof of the bed can be painted to complement the interior of the owner's home with a bespoke cushion for the pet. While the design provides shelter, the structure's frame allows for 360-degree views of the surrounding area, keeping the family pet involved in the daily workings of the home.

Name of Design:
Pet House Series
Name of Company:
Natural Slow

This series of beds is crafted from traditional Japanese Paulownia wood, favoured for being lightweight and durable, as well as being able to regulate temperatures and humidity. The Kamakura model, bottom right, takes its name from Japanese snow huts, the thirteen panels crafted to create a nostalgic, sheltered space. The Hokora, top right, with its polyhedron structure and triangular opening, creates a secluded space for cats that favour the quiet life; and for the pet that likes to bask in the sunshine, the Negura, below, features a pentagonal form that opens skywards and cradles the pet in a safe place.

Name of Design:
**Dog Unit Sheridan
Residence**
Name of Company:
StudioAC

The focus of the downstairs of this home renovation, undertaken by architecture firm StudioAC in Toronto, was to orient the family rooms around a singular focal point. This centrepiece is a large floor-to-ceiling plywood unit that divides the bottom floor into a foyer, a living and dining space, and a kitchen. It also contains storage units and hides the staircase. But, most importantly, it is the location of Rusty the dog's own little house. This fun design is propped against the plywood unit, with the simple gable-roofed den being painted white to complement the extended counter space that runs along the unit into the kitchen.

Name of Design:	The mpup Pet Furniture Collection by Seoul-based designer
Pet House	Seungji Mun was designed to create high-quality furniture for
Name of Designer:	dogs. With the number of pets joining families increasing every
Seungji Mun	year, Mun hopes to change the way interior design is conceived,

The mpup Pet Furniture Collection by Seoul-based designer
Seungji Mun was designed to create high-quality furniture for
dogs. With the number of pets joining families increasing every
year, Mun hopes to change the way interior design is conceived,
with pets receiving their own dedicated spaces. This elegant,
gable-roofed house is perfectly sized for a puppy or a medium-
sized dog. The simple structure consists of wooden slats, with
a ventilation panel at the back and two small handles on the side
for manoeuvrability. The floor can be lined with the Pet Bed
(p.197) from the same range.

Name of Design:
Retro
Name of Company:
WOHNBLOCK

This design by Oliver Kriege aims to please design-loving cat owners who are tired of unimaginative pet accessory designs. The sculpture-like structure also strives to fulfil the needs of the most beloved, high-maintenance, feline friends. At 1.75 metres (69 inches) tall, the tower is made of sturdy multiplex board with six ascending platforms, each lined with a durable carpet that provides comfortable support and grip – and is also perfect for having a nap on. Sisal boards run up the side of the tower, ready for a cat to scratch to its heart's content – saving the sofa from the worst of their efforts.

Name of Design:
Marron, Season 2
Name of Company:
Bad Marlon

South Korean company Bad Marlon Design Studio creates products that bring owners and pets closer together. This design from their 2017 range is the second edition of the hugely popular Marron bed. Assembling the structure is simple: the single piece of solid felt is flexed into a clam-like shape to form the structure, and brass buttons secure it in place via a bolt system. The partly covered bed is designed to embrace the pet, allowing the animal to feel psychologically and physically at ease – and the luxurious fluffy microfibre cushion provides them with the ultimate comfort.

Name of Design:
CATable 2.0
Name of Company:
LYCS Architecture

Having created the extremely successful CATable 1.0 (p.96) in search of a shared space for owner and cat, the modular 2.0 design endeavours to develop the idea, with the added benefit of being even more versatile. Consisting of equally-sized cubes, these wooden modules can be adapted to different needs, allowing the product to be used as a stool, coffee table or even a bookshelf. Each module contains an intriguing space or platform for a cat to stroll through, sleep in or cause havoc. The remaining space is available to fill with personal items; although as all cat-owners know, the cat's needs will always come first.

Name of Design:
Fishbowl
Name of Company:
Chimère Edition

This reimagining of the classic fishbowl comes from Bloom Room, the creative studio of Marc Ange. The Chimère Edition is a collection that draws on our collective subconscious of familiar designs and, with new and elegant concepts, sparks an excitement for these practical sculptures. Manufactured in Italy, the natural oak base with its smoothed edges stands on four legs, creating a friendly aesthetic demeanour. The blown glass bell jar with its circular air vent adds to the character of this design. The small scene at the bottom shows a carving of a galleon riding the waves, contrasting with the serene world of the fishbowl.

Name of Design:
Birdhouse
Name of Company:
CPOPP Workshop

Using the avian egg as inspiration for this bird house, the egg-shaped roost is elevated from the ground – evocative of how birds often safeguard their eggs in the tops of trees, or in the clefts of mountains. The three-legged, steel stand supporting the house borrows its smooth, 'stack-of-stick' appearance from CPOPP Workshop's Soft collection, which celebrates friendly architecture without sharp corners or edges. Originally made of hand-oiled walnut wood as a unique stand-alone piece, the design was modified to create a more practical, outdoor version made of hand-milled teak wood.

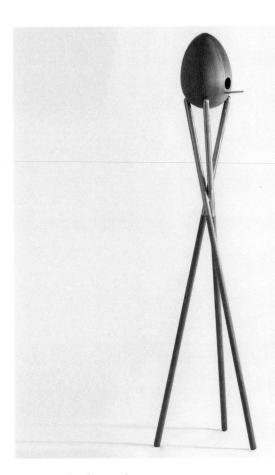

Name of Design:
CAnT WE ALL GET ALONG
Name of Company:
HKS

The renowned rivalries that cats have had with fish and birds, which stretch back millennia, may soon reach a friendly conclusion in this shelter, designed by HKS for the Giving Shelter fundraiser for stray cats. Within the confines of the wooden ribs of a large fish lies a hollowed interior for stray cats seeking respite from their tough lives on the street. Towering up and out of the fish are three multi-levelled bird houses, each with a gabled roof. The elevation of the bird houses helps the birds to find their perch, while sensibly keeping them just out of reach of their new furry companions.

This simple yet fun design is made entirely from white-coated recycled card. Almost any shape can be achieved with this transformable cat structure. The blocks slot together to create castles, forts, bridges or tunnels – meaning owner and cat can happily play together. Punched through the blocks are cat-sized holes and decorative patterns, allowing the sneakiest of felines to find spaces to hide. The blocks can be flat-packed for portability, and are easy to manipulate, yet strong enough to support several cats. Practical elements like a scratching post can also be added as desired.

Name of Design:
Hammock
Name of Designer:
Koichi Futatsumata

Designed by Koichi Futatsumata and produced by E&Y in Tokyo, this wicker hammock hangs in between the stainless steel frame and the glass top. Although this elegant coffee table was not originally designed for use by animals, it could be the perfect place for a cat to rest. The hammock itself is a symbol of relaxation that is protected by the glass, creating the effect of viewing an object through a shop window or museum showcase, accentuating the beautiful design – and beautiful pet. Positioned in a living area, the lucky cat would be right at the heart of the owner's daily life.

Name of Design:
D-Tunnel
Name of Designer:
Kenya Hara

With the aim of allowing smaller dogs to meet and greet their owners at eye level, this design from Kenya Hara of the Hara Design Institute is literally a raised platform. Joining the twelve other designs in the Architecture for Dogs initiative for Design Miami 2012, the D-Tunnel was built with a Teacup Poodle in mind and works as a 'scale modifier' to bring balance to the size difference between pet and owner. Constructed out of twelve timber panels and three bars joined together, the impressive structure creates an easy walkway for pets to connect at eye-level with their reclining owners.

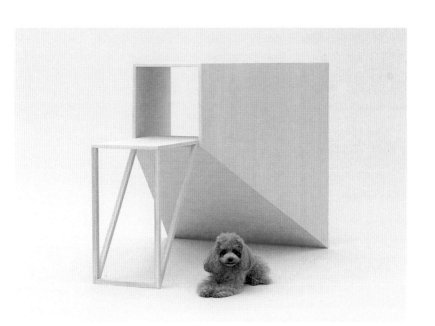

Ben Uyeda's HomeMade Modern is an online platform that aims to replace cheap store-bought designs, with natural and well-made goods that can be assembled at home. The DIY instructions are simple and easy to follow with step-by-step videos taking you through the process, and materials such as wood, steel and concrete make the designs cost-effective. This iconic house-shaped structure for a dog is made of Quikrete – a specially formulated high-strength concrete blend typically used for interior applications such as kitchen countertops. Once the concrete has set, a bed or rug can be placed inside for sleepy pets.

Name of Design:
Cat Tipi
Name of Designer:
Delphine Courier

This playful cat bed is made from lightweight but durable corrugated cardboard that is able to withstand even the most energetic cat's playtime. Assembled without the need for glue or tape, the transportable tipi simply clicks into shape and can be positioned anywhere. The entrance to the house is big enough for large cats, and has a second exit at the back, for cats that like a quick getaway opportunity. A third opening, a 'peek-a-boo' hole, sits on the side, offering cats the chance to spy on their surroundings. The design is available in numerous colours and patterns, to suit all types of interior.

"The greatness of a nation and its moral progress can be judged by the way its animals are treated."

Mahatma Gandhi

Name of Design:
ATOMO
Name of Company:
PetSuperfine

This striking, sculptural bed is equally strong, durable and beautiful. To form the structure, raw steel was manipulated by hand to create a sphere-like den, with the numerous geometric openings not only allowing light and air to flow through, but also enabling the family dog to keep an eye on their surroundings. The vibrant red cushion is fitted with a stain-resistant, removable cover that provides the perfect place for a dog to kick back and relax. Almost unnoticeable at the apex is a low voltage LED light emitting a soft, hazy light to calm and soothe after a long day on guard dog duty.

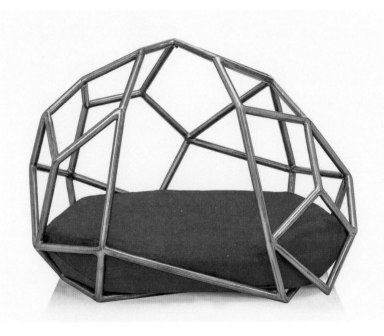

Name of Design:	Revising the archetypal form of the humble fish bowl,
Bubble Tank	designer Richard Bell of Psalt Design intended the Bubble Tank
Name of Designer:	to 'provoke a reaction, conversation or interaction between
Richard Bell	the owner and any guests'. Bell's design certainly achieves this;

the fish home protrudes over the surface it resides on, only just
supported by its counterbalanced weight, appearing like a water
drop that is about to run over the edge. Each Bubble Tank is
made to order, with the clear glass hand-blown and slumped to
create the overhang. Each tank is therefore unique, and has its
own character.

Name of Design:
Magis Dog House
Name of Designer:
Michael Young

This vibrant and playful dog house is suitable for both indoors and outdoors, due to the sturdy plastic that forms its core. Sitting on sleigh-like stainless steel legs, the house is elevated above ground, and features a protruding lip at its entrance, accessible by a set of steps filled with either sand or water to weigh it down. The curved, sloping roof extends over the opening to protect the porch – and residing pooch – from the elements. A simple brass plate above the door reads, *Amicus fidelis protectio fortis*, or, 'Faithful friend strong protector', for those owners that can't read Latin.

Name of Design:
Cat Shelter
Name of Company:
Perkins+Will

In recent years, architecture and design firm Perkins+Will have proved one of the most creative contributors to the annual Giving Shelter fundraiser for FixNation – the non-profit that spays, neuters and homes feral cats in and around Los Angeles. Their innovative designs for cat shelters (auctioned off for the charity) have included Catleidoscope (2016), UnFURled (2017) and, shown here, their 2014 contribution. An asymmetric design of 'stitched' and cantilevered triangular forms, its plastic, triple-entrance, weatherproof shell is lined with a paw-gripping fabric for ascending or descending feline occupants.

Name of Design:
Suite
Name of Company:
FORMA Italia

Italian design company Chiavari have been making bespoke and luxury furniture for close to fifty years. Their new FORMA Italia furniture line is focused solely on design for pets, and their mission is to set the standard for high quality, luxurious and elegant designs that are symbolic of a new way of cohabiting with animals. This splendid cat lounger features curved plywood, with a medium density lacquer and glossy varnish in Italian red and neutral white. It can be suspended by steel cables or sit atop metal feet. The retro-patterned soft cushion is cleverly kept in place by magnets.

Intending to redefine the relationship between human and dog, this inventive design for a Boston Terrier seeks to turn the family pet back into a proactive animal living alongside humans. The grid structure is made from *hinoki* (Japanese cypress wood), with transparent acrylic slats running through each cube, turning this structure into a series of shelves. While the internal hollowed-out space is solely for the dog, the surrounding shelves are the boundary between human and animal, to be used as storage for anything that gets used in daily life, positioning the dog as keeper of the most loved elements of the home.

Name of Design:
Pointed T
Name of Company:
Hara Design Institute

Designed for the Architecture for Dogs series that appeared at Design Miami in 2012, this brilliant shelter was conceived and created for the loyal Japanese Terrier. Simple yet striking, the Pointed T is made from a large sheet of coloured card with a cut-out entrance, and tape holds the edges together to complete the cone shape. The piece is suspended via a semi-transparent cord connected to the ceiling. Hovering above the ground, this floating teepee draws attention to the dog, becoming its very own designated space to sleep under or to guard from, while being the centrepiece of any owner's home.

Name of Design:
Cozy Pet House
Name of Company:
Curver

Inspired by the art of knitting, the Cozy Pet House is a design that is warm, familiar and nostalgic, comprising materials that are malleable and durable. Using injection moulding, the nest is actually manufactured out of of resin, coloured in a number of comforting tones. The result is this cosy knit-like texture that gives definition to the cat or small dog's personal space within the owner's home. The cushion can be placed inside or on the top, turning the house into a two-levelled bunk bed of sorts. The house can also be turned upside down to reveal more of the beautiful knit pattern.

Name of Design:
Bird House Rooftile
Name of Designer:
Klaas Kuiken

This terracotta bird's nest was developed by Designer Klaas Kuiken, in conjunction with Vogelbescherming Nederland – a Dutch organization promoting the protection of birds. Combining the humble bird house with a characteristic roof tile, this fun idea aims to arrest the declining urban bird population. Inside the bird house is a nesting basket made of wood and wire mesh that prevents the birds getting under other roof tiles, provides ventilation and makes the nest easy to clean after breeding season. A small wooden peg under the entrance provides a place to perch, so birds can get in and out of their roost more easily.

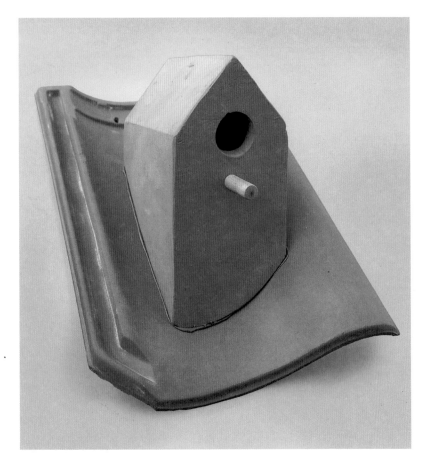

Name of Design:
Chihuahua Cloud
Name of Designers:
Jesse Reiser and
Nanako Umemoto

RUR Architecture PC's quirky yet sophisticated exoskeleton for a Chihuahua comprises three layers: the first encases the dog's joints, tracking its movements, the second is a structure of prosthetic elements that articulates the movements of the dog onto the outer and puffed-up third layer – the latter both warms and gives this small dog a much larger presence, in keeping with its personality. In addition, the integral lead from the Chihuahua's collar has the status of another limb, and one that symbolizes, through the give and pull of its fabric, the traditional relationship between pet and owner.

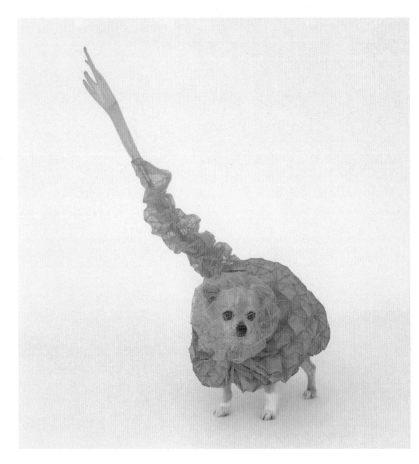

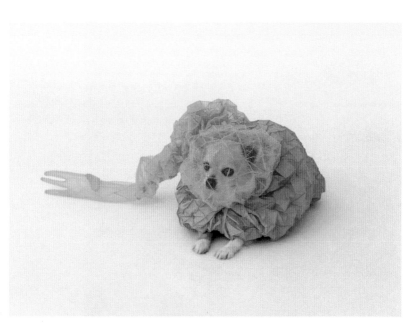

Name of Design:
Mija Beds
Name of Company:
WOWBOW London

Kim and Richard Bull, the designers and owners of WOWBOW, went through the familiar sequence of events of searching high and low for a suitable bed for their dog. Disappointed to find only poorly made beds covered in garish tartans and paw prints, they decided to create the Mija (pronounced mee-haa) line of pet designs. A rectangular acrylic base forms the structure of the bed, with the resting area lined with a lush cushion that is filled with memory foam, providing optimal, luxurious comfort. Solid and translucent colours for the frame and cushions are available to suit any home interior theme.

Name of Design:
Dogchitecture Dog House
Name of Company:
Bunker Arquitectura

The idea behind this vibrant design comes from the familiar action of a dog chasing its own tail: the entwined gable-roof resembles a large, overlapping ribbon, resulting in an elevated pathway, thereby creating a more interesting and dynamic runway – solely for a dog, of course. The design was Bunker Arquitectura's contribution to *Dogchitecture* – a travelling exhibition in Mexico, inviting designers to reinvent the archetypal dog's home. The exhibition was largely inspired by Kenya Hara's Architecture for Dogs project, which saw leading Japanese architects create DIY designs for dog owners.

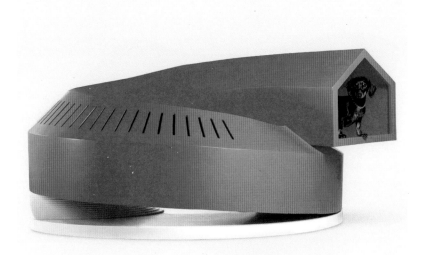

Name of Design:
Architecture for the Bichon Frise
Name of Designer:
Kazuyo Sejima

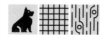

Kazuyo Sejima, co-founder of Japanese architecture firm SANAA, conceived of this DIY bed specifically for a Bichon Frise, as part of Kenya Hara's Architecture for Dogs initiative. Looking at the characteristic, fluffy texture of the breed's fur, the piece almost resembles a Bichon – a giant fluffy cloud. Sejima's design is only completed when the dog curls up into the bed – the architecture and animal merging to become one. MDF is cut into strips, formed into a ring and tied with string. A unique knitting method creates the fluffy exterior, and the small hole at the back of the design forms the Bichon's own private den.

Name of Design:
Feral Cat Shelter
Name of Company:
**Formation Association
with Edgar Arceneaux**

In collaboration with artist Edgar Arceneaux, Formation Association designed and donated this shelter for Los Angeles-based FixNation, a charity dedicated to spaying and neutering homeless cats. Not only does the shelter provide a place for cats to play and sleep, the structure doubles as a bench capable of seating several human friends. The multifunctional product was created using hundreds of wooden slats: the top of the bench is flat for sitting on, while the underbelly seems to ripple, as the ribs of the shelter undulate, creating an exciting and safe space for cats to hide in and climb through.

Name of Design:
Red-thread and Slatted Plywood Structure
Name of Company:
Stantec

Formerly known as RNL, architecture giant Stantec designed and manufactured this structure in aid of the Architects for Animals Giving Shelter charity fundraiser for FixNation – who work to trap-neuter-return cats in the San Fernando Valley, north of Los Angeles. The elegant plywood arch frames the periphery of the design, spanning across like a 'stretching feline', giving this open space a boundary. The wooden slat stage sits on a bed of faux fur, offering different places for cats to sleep. Woven into the bridge is a single red thread, beautifully unifying the piece and providing cats with their old playmate, string.

"Animals are such agreeable friends — they ask no questions, they pass no criticisms."

George Eliot

The ingenious designers at Nendo are behind this inspired design. The Heads or Tails dog bed combines the traditional forms of a dog house and a dog bed into this playful, versatile hybrid. When the dog cosies up inside the bed, it becomes a protective shelter. But if the animal jumps on top of it, it becomes their comfy beanbag or cushion. Made out of a soft artificial leather, the bed is available in black or white to complement most home interiors. The form of the design is made up of triangular panels that are connected in a polygonal mesh, easily allowing the dog to change the shape.

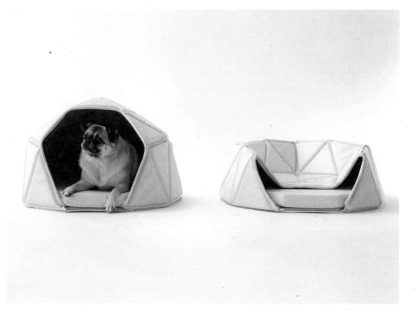

Made out of fibre-reinforced concrete, this 47 centimetre (18 inch) high bed is designed to be outside. The perfect size for a cat, this addition to the Concrete Garden collection, described by architect Tina Rugelj as a 'poetic garden collection', sits alongside the larger Concrete Dog House (p. 263). The thin shell is extremely light, but also durable – the reinforced material making the bed resistant to rain or even snow. The weathering of the exposed concrete is beautiful in its own right, with the imperfections and tarnishes from oxidation only adding to the character of this elegant, contemporary design.

Name of Design:
Alley Cats: HVAC edition
Name of Company:
D3architecture

Arminda Diaz of D3architecture created this cat shelter for the FixNation fundraiser Giving Shelter, which aims to raise money to help spay and neuter feral cats in Los Angeles. The piece was constructed out of materials found on the street, reflecting the harsh environment in which feral cats are forced to live. In the confines of a six foot cube steel frame, made out of a discarded heating, ventilation and air conditioning unit, a number of ducts are arranged to create refuge and passageways for the cats, with a sheltered wooden box at the centre offering a chance of secure respite from life on the streets.

Name of Design:
Snakerun
Name of Company:
Fuzzplay

Owner of Fuzzplay, Tobias Oberleithner seeks to inject a bit of playfulness back into our pets' lives, by turning open plan interiors into a more adventurous playground, filled with sophisticated shapes and areas for pets to enjoy. Using only heat-pressed felt and wooden buttons, these two-dimensional pieces of felt (when they arrive) can be turned into exciting designs for both pet and owner. By rolling the felt strips into a tunnel, they can be connected together with the buttons. The snake-like, moveable joints allow for a helpful, or playful, hand to interact with the cat, strengthening the human-animal bond.

Name of Design:
Cats in Style
Name of Designer:
Marly Gommans

Handmade in the Netherlands by designer Marly Gommans, the Cats in Style range is designed for cats that demand a little more privacy. Using natural and cat-friendly materials such as sisal and felt, the collection consists of a scratching post, a bed, a litter box and even a built-in cat flap for an interior door. The unique cross-shape featured on these pieces provides the cat with an opportunity for peace, quiet and privacy when doing their business or curling up for a nap, with the cat free to roam the house through closed doors without the owner having to repeatedly get up and open them.

Name of Design:
Birdhaus
Name of Company:
Claesson Koivisto Rune

Design collective OTHR have gathered the world's best designers to create unique, practical and stylish designs that have a minimal impact on the environment. One of the resulting innovations was the Birdhaus, conceived by the Swedish architecture and design firm Claesson Koivisto Rune. The idea for this simple reworking of the archetypal birdhouse came from the fact that a single bird can consume up to 3,500 mosquitos a day: 'making it an efficient, lyrical bug repeller for your home.' The inner and outer shells are ingeniously made of 3D-printed porcelain, in gloss white or matt black.

Name of Design:
Baco
Name of Company:
Brando Design

Sitting on stainless steel legs like a little creature in its own right, this woven wicker module is an ideal design for cats due to the rough claw-resisting texture of its body. The cocoon-like bed provides a comfy place for a cat to sleep and to observe, with the fine gaps in the wicker allowing the pet to spy on their neighbours. To be closer to the ground, the smooth steel legs can be removed, and fixed lengthways against the undercarriage. The two openings at either end of the pod are ideal for pet and owner to communicate with each other, with the cat feeling secure in having another way to escape.

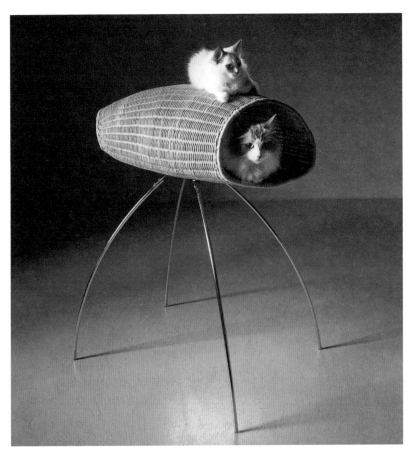

Name of Design:
Riva
Name of Company:
Laboni

Nominated for the 2018 German Design Award, the Riva pet bed was designed by Friederike Erhorn of Laboni. It excels not only in its pure and aesthetically pleasing form, but also in its innovative use of materials. The underlying frame is hand-welded from a lightweight aluminium alloy, while the polypropylene fabric woven like rope around it is filled with quick dry foam. The latter, together with the water-repellent qualities of the removable and washable cover, make this bed-basket suitable for both indoor and outdoor use. Cocoon-like for the occupant, it provides both psychological and physical comfort.

Name of Design:
Howly
Name of Company:
Howlpot

'We stand for companion animals' design rights' is the credo of the South Korean design firm Howlpot. Re-evaluating the relationship between pet and owner, they seek to raise the standard of pet products to match the quality of our human furnishings by focusing primarily on the comfort of the pet, and using luxurious materials. The Howly is easily assembled by inserting the circular steel frame into the mouth of the fabric, creating an open shelter. The outer material is made of a mixture of polyester and cotton and is available in a number of attractive pastel colours, with the inside cushion covered in a water-resistant material.

Name of Design:
Cat Bed
Name of Company:
Tateno Woodheart
Studio

This cat bed was designed and produced by master craftsmen in the Fukuoka prefecture of Japan is Okawa-shi, an area famous for woodwork and furniture-making for the last 500 years. Designed in the tradition of bonsai miniatures, this bed emulates the shape and style of the owner's bed, except on a perfectly formed, smaller scale. The natural wood finish is designed to age and 'shine' as cats rub against the bed – and be treasured for many years to come, just like any other piece of furniture. All that is needed to complete the look are tiny pillows and a mattress, and a happy cat looking for a stylish place to have a nap.

Name of Design:
Cat-à-Tête
Name of Company:
Formation Association

This cat-inspired tête-à-tête by Formation Association, in collaboration with Arktura and BuroHappold, was conceived for the Architects for Animals Giving Shelter initiative – fundraising for non-profit FixNation, who work to neuter and spay feral cats. The sheeting used is made from recycled plastic bottles and has a fibrous quality that gives the surfaces a felt-like feel. The material is repeatedly layered in a figure-of-eight form, encouraging an ongoing dialogue between seated humans and cats who, via the numerous entrances and exits to the enclosed shelter below, can come and go as they please.

Name of Design:
Teepee
Name of Company:
Hellopets

Handmade in Poland, this fun little 90 centimetre (35 inch) high pet bed is simply constructed out of four wooden poles, with soft grey felt enclosing and enveloping the frame. A narrow strip of felt is wrapped around the crossed poles at the top of the teepee to keep them in place. The trapezoid-shaped entrance keeps the bed open, lit and ventilated, while still providing a sense of privacy and protection – just perfect for the pet that likes to snuggle up while keeping an eye on their territory. The square-shaped base is lined with felt, but is large enough to take a soft pillow for the more demanding pet.

Name of Design:
Modular Wall Climber
Name of Company:
DOTE

This all-vegan design is manufactured almost entirely of recycled materials. It came from the designer's drive to make smart, stylish and eco-friendly designs that are also practical for cats. Using recycled tubing and a wall bracket, heat-pressed felt is wrapped around the modules, creating this modern and sleek wall climber. Designed with the urban cat in mind, the climber provides more surface area in the home, encouraging the cat to climb, play and exercise. Because felt is a favourite material for many cats, the climber is perfect for a good scratch, or even a cosy nap up high.

Name of Design:
Dog House Sofa
Name of Designer:
Seungji Mun

With more than ten million pets being raised in South Korea, the image of the modern nuclear family is seldom seen without a dog or a cat. The new mpup range, of which the Dog House Sofa is a part, is a collection looking to bridge the gap between human and animals, by bringing them together via this multipurpose sofa. Made of solid ash wood, this clever piece of furniture sees the classic sofa combined with the sheltered doghouse. The small gap between the seat and the dog shelter encourages interaction between pet and owner, while making sure the dogs feel they have a space to make their own.

"Some of my best leading men
have been dogs and horses."

Elizabeth Taylor

Name of Design:
CATable 1.0
Name of Company:
LYCS Architecture

This piece of furniture from the LYCS design team was inspired by their experiences of living with a cat. The aptly named CATable is designed for both cat and owner to share. The first experience the designers focused on was having to move a cat from a laptop when trying to work, describing this act as 'a sentimental ritual of temporary farewell'. The second is a cat's limitless curiosity in exploring the unknown. The holes and beautiful pathways through the table provide an adventure for the cat, while allowing the owner to work in peace, meaning they never have to say goodbye.

Name of Design:
Living with Pet
Name of Company:
Deesawat

Thailand-based design company Deesawat, specializing in woodwork, has created Living with Pet, an indoor and outdoor sofa for pets. The frame is made out of teak wood, perfect for outdoor furniture, with the light fabric that encases the top and sides working as a sunscreen and wind buffer. With the changing perception of pets in family environments, this design sees pets as real members of the family, seeking to adapt conventional furniture to suit a new lifestyle. A specific space for the pet is made in the form of the interchangeable modular box, allowing pet and owner to spend time together, strengthening their bond.

Name of Design:
Black Frame Fence
Name of Company:
Bad Marlon

The objective of all designs by Bad Marlon Design Studio, based in South Korea, is to create an environment for pet and owner alike that shares a same-design-identity: a space that respects the cohabitation of human and animal, strengthening the owner-pet bond. This minimalist dog pen is made up of a series of plywood bars and coloured Eco Board modules connected together via clips, allowing it to be extended, perfect for the home or a larger social setting. The fence stands 73 centimetres (29 inches) high and contains a plywood door with a bolt lock to provide access, and keep the pen secure.

Name of Design:
Dew Drop Bird Box
Name of Company:
**Peter Lanyon
Furniture**

Plymouth-based bespoke furniture maker Peter Lanyon has crafted this delightful nest for garden birds. The wood is sourced from locally grown birch and sweet chestnut trees, and is fashioned into either a small or a large 'dew drop' box. The smaller size will meet the requirements of tree sparrows, tits and European pied flycatchers, with the larger nest suiting sparrows, nuthatches and starlings. The wood is then layered with a protective finish and a UV protecting oil to preserve this beautiful bird home for years to come. To remove old nests and clean the box, a small door at the rear grants access to the interior.

Name of Design:
Pet Teepee
Name of Company:
Wild and Loyal

The Montreal-based designers of this adventurous indoor teepee were intent on creating a comfortable space for pets that complemented domestic interiors with a unique design. Fashioned from one hundred per cent cotton canvas fabric, the structure is held in place by solid wooden poles. Predominantly off-white, the piece is accented with black stripes at the base, black crosses above the triangular opening, and is finished with black pole tips. Soft plush cushions adorned with arrows on the inside make this heroic teepee attractive to the wildest of cats and the craziest of dogs.

Name of Design:
Ball of Twine
Name of Company:
**Abramson Teiger
Architects**

This joyful design was made for the annual Giving Shelter fundraiser for FixNation, a charity working to neuter and spay stray cats in Los Angeles, which sees the top architects and designers in the area design shelters for the city's stray cats. This beautifully simple cat shelter resembles an enlarged ball of twine, and is aptly made from the same material. The spherical shelter contains a small opening, with little gaps in the twine to provide light and ventilation. The base is also wrapped in string, providing support for the shelter, but mainly offering the cats something to play with.

Name of Design:
Nest
Name of Company:
Krab

Boxes: cats love them. A place that is safe and secure, enclosed except for an opening that allows observation of their surroundings, and even a quick getaway. Drawing on this, Wout and Nikita – the owners and designers of Krab – crafted the first 'nest' for cats. Inside this luxury poplar plywood box is a soft feather-light pillow made of faux fur. Adorned on the side is the 'Rising Sun' sneak hole that depicts the rays of a sunrise, while permitting light and sound in, as well as allowing a sneaky view of the outside. The minimalist design makes it perfect for owners' needs as well, doubling as a side table.

Name of Design:
Nogg
Name of Designers:
**Matthew Hayward
and Nadia Turan**

Resembling a large egg, this modern chicken coop by Matthew Hayward and Nadia Turan houses up to four chickens. Made from sustainably sourced cedar wood, the Nogg is naturally resistant to bacteria, while emitting a fresh and natural scent. The entrance to the coop blends in with the cedar panels, but is reinforced with a stainless steel frame to protect the outdoor coop from wear and tear from the elements. A circular twisting glass top can be lifted to aid ventilation and provide a view of the goings-on in the roost. The coop sits on a concrete base, keeping it stable and damp-proof.

Name of Design:
Catosphere
Name of Company:
**Standard
Architecture**

The Architects for Animals Giving Shelter initiative draws upon the best architects and designers in Los Angeles to create shelters for feral cats seeking refuge from the elements. The project is in aid of FixNation, a not-for-profit organization that helps spay and neuter feral cats. Resting on brass legs is this beautiful concrete pod. The thermal conducting properties allow the capsule to absorb heat throughout the day, and slowly release it through the night. A warm pet bed sits in the middle of the pod, with the encircling louvred wood walls regulating the airflow and light coming in and out of the structure.

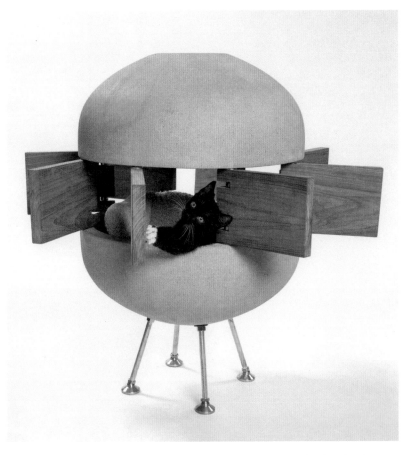

Name of Design:
**MiaCara Torre Cat
Scratching Post**
Name of Designer:
Regina Mol

For a cat, scratching is an important part of life. The physical efforts of working their muscles and stretching, and filing those sharp claws, are extremely beneficial. This scratching post addresses this need and, at the same time, saves your sofa. Inspired by the philosophy of 'form follows function', Dutch designer Regina Mol has encased one of the plywood panels (available in either oak or walnut) in needle felt, popular for its resistance to claws. Set on a stable circular base of solid wood, the overhead platform is perfect for the cat that likes to keep an eye on its surroundings.

Name of Design:
Elevator B
Name of Designers:
University at Buffalo students

Standing at 6.7 metres (22 feet) tall, this skyscraper is home to a colony of bees. Made by architecture students at the University at Buffalo, the design is enveloped in a honeycomb of stainless steel sheets, protecting the interior containing the wooden box that houses the bees. Small triangles were punctured into the panels to allow in shafts of light. Near the top of the tower, the bees are accomodated in a hexagonal wooden 'bee cab' that works as an elevator, allowing the beekeepers to pulley down the colony for inspection and maintenance. Visitors can view the hive through the tower's laminated glass base.

Name of Design:
Curvynest Cat Tree
Name of Company:
Catswall Design

The concept for this curving nest for cats came from the idea of 'piled tunnels', and results in a safe and designated space for numerous cats. Constructed of MDF board and PVC woven fabric, the Curvynest has an elastic nature that creates a subtle bouncing action when jumped on, turning each curve into a sort of cradle for the cat. The four storeys are enclosed enough to give each cat their own elevated private space, with the woven lining ideal for grip and scratching alike. The design bends and curves upwards to the uppermost horizontal platform that is excellent for observation and interacting with people.

Name of Design:
Inside Dog House
Name of Company:
Sauder

The Sauder Pet Home Collection features a number of attractive and playful products, that cater first for pets' needs, but are also the pinnacle of practicality. One such item in the collection is this indoor dog den that is designed for small to medium-sized dogs. The house features a comfortable fabric bed with a removable, washable cover, plus an attached porch protruding out under the roof. This gable roof contains an indented shelf to store essential items, with a food and water shelf extending from the side. Attached to the rear of the house is a large pole to store the lead, ready for those all-important walks.

Name of Design:
Honey Factory
Name of Designer:
Francesco Faccin

This hive by Francesco Faccin, made in collaboration with professional beekeeper Mauro Veca, stands as a beacon to raise public awareness of the serious problem of declining bee populations. The unit is designed for urban areas, and can even be located on top of city roofs. The bees are kept safe at the top of the big 'chimney'; the large glass door protects the hive, while providing a view of the colony at work. The infamous bee 'waggle dance' (a sort of figure-of-eight movement that instructs the hive where to find pollen and nectar) can be glimpsed, allowing people to learn, empathize, and lose their fear of these insects.

This fully customizable tower works as a play area for cats, as well as a display shelf for the owner. Comprising movable boxes and platforms, this towering cat tree looks great in any surrounding, be it a plant-filled conservatory, or a book-lined library. Each shelf has a lining of fine carpet to provide comfort and a more stable launching and landing pad, with the three adjustable boxes being small, in line with a cat's preference for exploring nooks and crannies. The main body of the Necobaco is treated with resin in order to protect from cat scratches and general wear and tear.

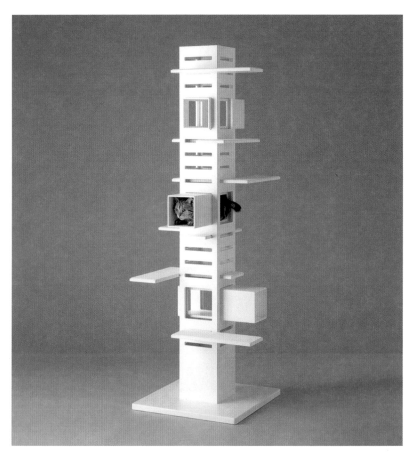

Name of Design:
Katris
Name of Company:
Papercut Lab

All those years of playing Tetris are about to pay off. The Papercut Lab team, based in California, specialize in all things paper – they love it for its endless design possibilities, as well as its environmental credentials. The act of scratching is an important workout for indoor cats, and these Tetris-inspired modules are formed using layered corrugated cardboard, one of the best surfaces for cats to scratch due to its robust nature that offers tough resistance against claws. The modularity of the piece is important, allowing the structures to suit various interiors, and creating new explorative routes for a cat.

Knowing that cats always like to nap in places they shouldn't, this simple and elegant design from South Korean company Purr provides the perfect place for a cat to recline. Reminiscent of a traditional washing basket, the frame is made of sturdy powder-coated steel, with small rubber clips that can be attached to stop the base from moving. The designated cat hammock fits into the frame, allowing the feline to get snug within the cocoon of the canvas sling. The easily portable and open-top Raf is ideal for cats that like to soak up the rays when positioned in a warm patch of sun.

Name of Design:
Hutch
Name of Company:
Chimère Edition

Looking to buy a good-looking hutch for his goddaughter's rabbit, Frédéric Stouls enquired with friend and designer Marc Ange on where he could purchase such an item. Unable to find anything suitable, the two friends decided to create a range of pieces boasting a timeless beauty. Made in Ange's studio, Bloom Room, and drawing upon the simplicity and quality of Scandinavian design, the Hutch was born. The solid oak hutch is elevated on four legs with lacquered feet. The entrance opens to a sleeping area, which leads to a walkway ascending to a platform. A ceramic rabbit head adorns the facade.

Name of Design:
Cat-a-Comb
Name of Company:
Atelier Suburban

Drawing on a cat's love of safe and enclosed spaces, the aptly named Cat-a-Comb by Irina Dragomir and Bogdan Ispas of Atelier Suburban is a small and cozy feline shelter. The structure is made of birch plywood, the layered edges of the exterior contrasting with its teardrop shape. Simulating the natural resting places of domestic cats, such as in cardboard boxes or on top of bookshelves, the piece looks to suit all cat characters, with the design allowing them to reside on the floor or be hung from the ceiling. A small peephole is incorporated into the side, making cats feel safer with increased sightlines.

"Let us remember that animals are not mere resources for human consumption. They are splendid beings in their own right, who have evolved alongside us as co-inheritors of all the beauty and abundance of life on this planet."

Marc Bekoff

Name of Design:
Non-slip Bird House
Name of Company:
Nendo

Nendo's Non-slip Bird House is one of the ten designs commisioned for the *Can You Imagine* exhibition at the National Museum of 21st Century Arts (MAXXI) in Rome, which saw ten projects created using the material Alcantara. One of the qualities of Alcantara is its suede-like texture that gives it a non-slip surface – frequently used on car seats to keep a driver positioned upright. Focusing on this characteristic of the material, the designers were able to attach numerous Alcantara gable-roofed bird houses on to a large, slopping wall of the same material, without glue or screws, relying solely on friction.

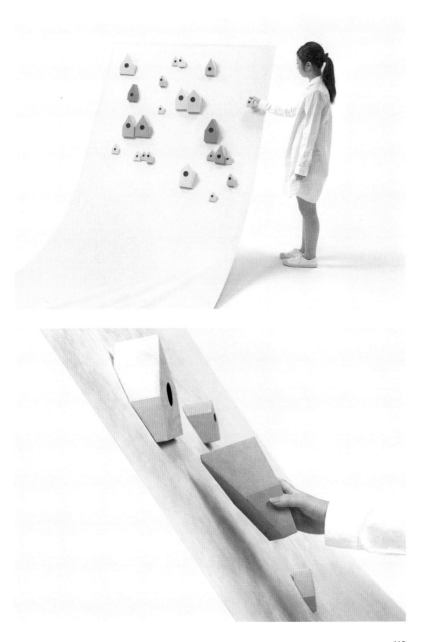

Name of Design:
Fishbowls
Name of Designer:
Roger Arquer

These elegant fish bowls are from a series of fifteen concepts that deviate from the archetypal bowl by introducing a moral or practical aspect, questioning standard designs for pet fish. The Bottle Vase (below) makes us consider how we can repurpose old objects, such as a vase, for fish habitation. The XS or XL (top right) explores the relationship between a big and a small fish cohabiting. The Chill Out/Warm Up (bottom right) allows water temperature to be regulated by adding hot water or ice via the corked receptacle. They are made from borosilicate glass, commonly use for laboratory equipment.

Name of Design:
Shelter for Hermit Crabs
Name of Artist:
Aki Inomata

Artist Aki Inomata's idea to provide hermit crabs with a shelter was inspired by the *No Man's Land* exhibition in 2009, at the French Embassy in Japan. That year, the French handed back their embassy land to the Japanese. Although the land will be returned to the French in fifty years time, the temporary arrangement symbolizes peace and cooperation. Made of 3D-printed resin, Inomata's work of art shelters take the form of cities around the world, playing with the idea of exchanging nationalities, crossing borders, and giving a sense of identity for migrants and refugees.

Name of Design:
Parole
Name of Designers:
**Leopold Banchini and
Daniel Zamarbide**

The Parole cage is able to house a large number of mice, but the real reason for its construction was not so much the practical element, but the ethical quandaries it poses. It raises the question of the role of the architect when asked to design something as morally ambiguous as a prison, and furthermore how their skills can create something that encourages debate. The Parole cage is modelled on the Geneva prison Champ-Dollon, known for its maximum occupancy numbers. The design is scaled down for laboratory mice, to stimulate a moral and political response to living conditions.

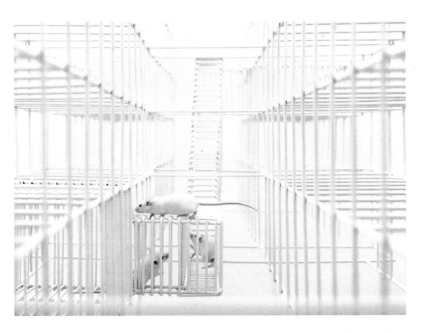

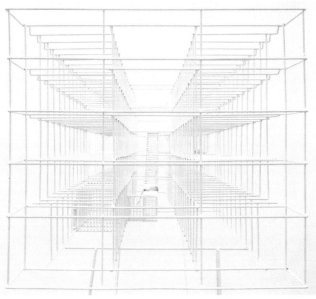

Joining the other brilliant designs of the Giving Shelter charity fundraiser for FixNation, whose work involves neutering and spaying feral cats in Los Angeles, comes this shelter from leading global design and architecture firm HOK. Wrapping around the seven chambers is a faux-wood cover that is built to withstand the most adverse weather conditions, contrasting with the fluffy interior that is lined with felt and other fabrics, keeping the shelter warm and comfortable. With multiple cats able to be housed, each chamber contains a circular exit hole at the back, perfect for a quick getaway.

Name of Design:
AIR 1 Aquarium
Name of Designer:
Amaury Poudray

French designer Amaury Poudray uses simple elements to create beautiful furniture, using a combination of materials to construct items that test the boundaries of design. Seemingly hovering in the air like a Zeppelin, this glass fish tank for Siamese fighting fish – more commonly known as betta fish – is supported on simple steel rods that are secured into the aquarium through two small slots in the glass. For Amaury, creating a habitat for a living creature, combined with the simple materials and flowing shapes, the design is reminiscent of the art of writing, which 'combines letters to create meaning.'

Name of Design:
The Cat Mod Complex
Name of Company:
Catastrophic
Creations

These modular complexes for cats are bursting with creativity in their designs. The Indiana Jones-inspired structures are completely modular, allowing pathways to be formed in a wide variety of patterns. The wooden platforms are mounted to a wall via hidden brackets, allowing them to appear to float, with the washable cotton canvas walkways perfect for adventuring or even sleeping. The rope cat bridge is safely supported by tough paracord with the railing along the bridge woven from rustic twine. The complex offers more surface space in a home for a cat, and more perches to watch the world go by.

129

Name of Design:
Hepper Pod Pet Bed
Name of Company:
Hepper

This futuristic pod by founder and creative director of Hepper, Jed Crystal, is supported on a silver steel frame, with the fabric made of black-and-white Herringbone, and a soft sherpa fleece and microfibre lining for the interior. It was designed to provide a place for 'perfect cat naps' while also being an attractive design for any home interior. The lid can be removed to create a day bed for cats who like to recline in more open settings, keeping an eye on their surroundings. With the top on, the pod creates a warm and safe environment with an opening large enough to ventilate the interior.

Name of Design:
The Darwin Tank
Name of Company:
The Darwin Sect

The otherworldly beauty of jellyfish is undeniable. Their soft pulsing movements and tranquil floating give them an ethereal quality. Florence Samain and Dave Monfort formed The Darwin Sect to showcase the beauty of nature, while supporting environmental organizations. The dome is formed of durable and transparent glass designed for laboratory use, and is similar in design to the Napoleon III domes used in Charles Darwin's time. The filter and pump are hidden beneath the tank, with the water gently filtered, leaving a crystal clear tank like a 'drop of the ocean in your living room'.

These stunning bird cages depict three of the most distinguished museum and art exhibition spaces in the world. Below is a model of the New Museum in New York designed by SANAA. Top right is a model of the Guggenheim Museum in New York designed by Frank Lloyd Wright, with the bottom right being the São Paulo Museum of Art designed by Lina Bo Bardi. These stainless steel cages by artist Marlon de Azambuja were not specifically designed as habitats for birds, but resulted from his passion for contemporary art and design, the two disciplines overlapping in these remarkable pieces to accomodate birds.

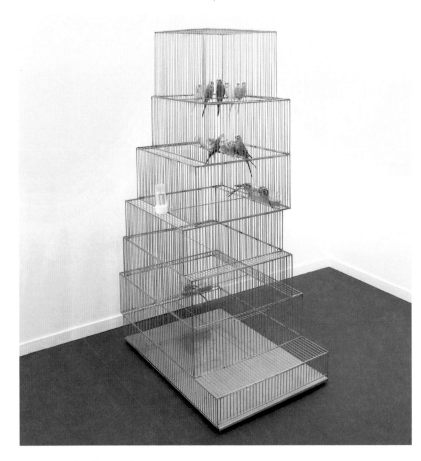

133

"Some people talk to animals.
Not many listen though.
That's the problem."

A. A. Milne

Name of Design:
Papier Papillon
Name of Designer:
Shigeru Ban

This free-flowing design by Japanese architect Shigeru Ban is part of renowned product designer Kenya Hara's Architecture for Dogs initiative, an inspired collection of designs for dogs that can be made at home by following online tutorials or printable blueprints. By simply manipulating common paper tubes, such as those found at the centre of a roll of bubble wrap, numerous shapes can be made. The tube is drilled at either end, with soft wire threaded through and tied off at the ends, creating a delicate undulating structure that can be turned into a series of mazes for a dog, a pet bed or even a comfy chair for the owner.

Name of Design:
**Natural Sphere
Cat Tower**
Name of Company:
Sauder

Acknowledging the need for cats to have a place to unwind, as well as play, this structure claims to be the perfect tower for felines. Topped with a two-door wicker sphere that houses a cosy cushion, the tower is supported on three legs made of wood with an espresso-coloured finish. The carpeted raised platform is the perfect place from which to attack the toy dangling from the base of the sphere by an elastic string. Knowing how important it is for domestic cats to get their exercise, one of the legs is encased in sisal rope, the perfect material to encourage cats to scratch, which stretches and works their muscles.

Name of Design:
Architecture for
Long-Bodied,
Short-Legged dog
Name of Company:
Atelier Bow-Wow

Joining the Architecture for Dogs series – the initiative commissioned by the Hara Design Institute and Nippon Design Centre for Design Miami in 2012 – comes this ramp system by Japanese architects Atelier Bow-Wow. Built for the short-legged Smooth Dachshund, the structure allows these small dogs to walk up the connecting slopes and reach eye level with their seated owner – much easier than stairs. Comprising timber panels, the walkways link to open-ended platforms that can be added or removed, forming various levels the dog can reach, or instead creating parallel benches for dog and owner alike.

Name of Design:
Petting Farm
Name of Company:
70F Architecture

The governing body of the city of Almere in the Netherlands commissioned the construction of a new children's petting farm in Uylpark. This automated enclosure was built on the foundations of a previous petting zoo. Enveloped in wooden slats, the facade's automatic wooden shutters open up in response to natural light and, in turn, close after the sun sets – making this farm wake up and go to sleep just like its inhabitants. The high-ceilinged stable opens on to a field surrounded by gates where the public can feed the animals. A hay loft, public conveniences and a meeting room make up the rest of this public petting farm.

Name of Design:
Nest Nº1
Name of Designer:
Filippo Pisan

Italian design company De Castelli produced this elegant, minimalist reworking of the typical bird house. It is made of weathering, or Cor–Ten steel, which is known for its beautiful rust-like appearance after several years' exposure to the elements. The fir wood front and rear complete this pentagonal-shaped nest, with a small hole providing entry to the roost. The designer, Filippo Pisan, created a similar structure for humans called Cottage Nº1, which is larger at 2.4 metres (7 ft 8 inches) tall. Drawing on centuries of experience, the company is known for work that incorporates steel, wood and stone in pleasingly aesthetic designs.

Name of Design:
Dew Drop Bee Home
Name of Company:
**Peter Lanyon
Furniture**

Solitary bees, like the Leafcutter and Mason bee, have a tough time finding nooks and crannies in today's modern architecture. When it comes to having a rest or laying eggs, a narrow tunnel with a single opening – just like these bee nests made from bamboo shoots – is perfect. The shoots are simply bundled up and encased in a sheet of locally grown birch plywood, forming this charming teardrop-shaped home for bees. The wood is treated with a UV-resistant oil to protect it from the elements, and the homes are designed to attract a variety of bees and insects helping to pollinate the garden.

Sander, Joost and Maarten formed Drievrienden – the Dutch for 'three friends' – after meeting at architecture school in Delft. In the hunt for the perfect scratching post for their cats and for their interiors, they realized that whatever they ended up buying wouldn't be nearly as attractive to their cats as the cardboard box it came in. An idea was born. Krabhuis – the Dutch for 'scratch house' – combines the designers' architectural skills with a cat's love for cardboard. The design aims to offer a fun environment for a cat to play in, hide in or have a good nap in – keeping the owner's sofa scratch-free.

Name of Design:
BoxKitty
Name of Designers:
**John Wilson and
Edward Lim**

Why do cats do it? Their owners assemble large cumbersome pieces of cat furniture specially bought for them, they turn around and the cat has proudly nestled in their new home: the cardboard box it came in. Designers John Wilson and Edward Lim decided to take action. The design is comprised of individual cardboard panels with a variety of different perforations, some larger openings for entrances, smaller ones for windows, even a turret-shaped piece to make a castle for the more regal cat. The pieces connect via reusable tabs that hook and loop around, making the construction possibilities endless.

145

Name of Design:
Feline Sofa
Name of Company:
Hiromatsu Furniture

The Hiromatsu Furniture company, who specialize in wood work, are responsible for this outstanding piece of craftsmanship. They fall under the banner of the Okawa Furniture Collective, whose work depends on extremely skilled craftsmen to create furniture that will enrich the lives of its users. Each sofa is completely handmade from pinewood sourced from the Rocky Mountains. The corners of the wood are gently sanded down, giving the sofa an aged and worn look. Completing the vintage appearance, the four cushions are upholstered in a soothing olive green fabric.

Inspired by the natural attraction cats have to straw, and their own cat Tabby's fondness of beds made of natural materials, the Blink designers created the NekoHut. They drew on elements of the traditional cathouses of Japan, so each bed is handwoven with dried straw using the traditional *Neko Chigura* weaving technique (a pattern prevalent in Japanese basket design), giving the bed a homely quality. Handcrafted with renewable materials makes this bed eco-friendly, and brings the modern cat closer to nature. Resembling a small hut, the square opening of the NekoHut reveals a perfect place to rest.

Name of Design:
Catissa Cat House
Name of Company:
Catissa

Ilshat Garipov of Catissa created this wall-mounted cat house using four wooden modules and a ladder, and designed it for the cats who like to sleep and play above the hustle and bustle of normal life on the ground. Enclosed by five panels of smooth plywood, the cubes can be stacked on top of each other and each have cut-out windows and feline-sized gaps, creating numerous places for cats to climb through and look down from. Available in various water-based paint colours, each module is completed with either a sheepskin or faux-fur cushion that fits into the base of each box.

Name of Design:
Bat Tower
Name of Company:
Ants of the Prairie

Aiming to raise awareness of the importance of bats to our ecosystem, this bold and striking structure resembles a gargantuan sleeping bat. The plywood slats that make up the structure have grooves worked into the wood to make it easier for bats to cling to the tower and hang from the ceiling. Near the top of this clever construction are a number of landing pads that help facilitate access to the tower, and the dark wooden panels that cover the roof just over the 'inhabitation zone' absorb the heat from sunlight. Located next to a lake, the bats have access to all the insects they could ever want.

Name of Design:
MAO'er Hutong
Name of Company:
Okamoto Deguchi
Design

Fitting neatly between the ridges of traditional Chinese roof tiles, these wooden quarter-cylindrical modules were created to improve the quality of life for the cats that frequent the roofs of the *hutongs* (alleyways) in Beijing. The V-shaped cat shelters were submitted for Beijing Design Week in 2014. The sustainable and ecological wooden modules act as cat shelters, which also protect the old tiles from weeds that grow in abundance along the Dashilar district's skyline, causing erosion and decay. The lower opening works as the unit's drainage system with holes that allow water to run through.

Name of Design:
Birdwalk
Name of Company:
ODDO Architects

Inspired by the glamour and grace of a catwalk, this design by ODDO Architects has turned the humble bird feeder into an elevated catwalk for birds. Deviating from classic designs for bird feeders, this sleek and striking wooden structure is supported on three metal legs with a platform protruding from under the gable-roofed cover, providing ample opportunities for bird-watchers to glimpse a variety of species, such as robins, black-birds, blue jays and goldfinches, strut their stuff. A small circular window is positioned on the side of the roof, allowing the birds to take a peek at their surroundings.

"Animals are reliable, many full of love, true in their affections, predictable in their actions, grateful and loyal. Difficult standards for people to live up to."

Alfred A. Montapert

Name of Design:
catHAUS
Name of Company:
SPACE International

Sitting proudly like a miniature Mid-Century Modern house, this design comes from the Architects for Animals Giving Shelter fundraiser event for FixNation, a charity working to neuter and spay feral cats in Los Angeles. The structure operates as both human chaise longue and animal shelter, and was designed to be a retreat for feral cats while being a practical piece of furniture. The simple and elegant white lacquered wood exterior contrasts with the vibrant and playful synthetic grass that lines the gabled ceiling and floor. The platforms are suspended on cords of sisal rope, with elastic cord partitioning off the cat's space.

This retro-modernist-inspired design is available in two different materials: wood and plexiglass. The CAT60 shown here is made from natural elm wood finished with a scratch-resistant oil, with stainless steel legs to support the rectangular prism. Alternatively it can be attached directly to a wall. The curvilinear holes that are found around the structure are reminiscent of 1960s interior design, with the added benefit of allowing the cat to monitor their surroundings. With two open sides to this large bed, a comfortable cushion can be placed inside, with the openness encouraging more interaction between pet and owner.

Name of Design:
The Cat Cube
Name of Designer:
Delphine Courier

Unable to find an attractive bed for her cat, Delphine Courier looked to design the perfect piece of furniture that would suit the interior of her flat, while satisfying the high demands of her pet. Cardboard, being a popular choice among cats, was perfect for her pet to sit and sleep on, to rub against and to scratch. Not only is the material lightweight and sturdy, it is one hundred per cent recyclable, making this cat house completely eco-friendly. The design's icosahedron shape was chosen for what Delphine describes as its 'looks comfy' vibe, with the enclosed space perfect for her cat to get cosy.

Name of Design:
The Moop
Name of Company:
Nottoscale

This modern and stylish chicken coop is made for the urban garden. Designed for four hens, weathered plywood makes up the gable roof, with treated redwood panels forming the walls. Openings between the slats ventilate the interior while protecting the chickens from the elements. The sides of the elevated coop can be lowered in order to retrieve eggs. The two mesh runs can be configured in various ways, depending on the size of the available space. This modular chicken coop (or Moop) was built with the principles of prefabricated architecture in mind, making the flat-packed design practical and easy to assemble.

Name of Design:
Earth Cat Survivor
Name of Company:
Knowhow Shop

The designers of Knowhow Shop contributed this design to the Architects for Animals' inaugural Giving Shelter charity event – fundraising for FixNation, a charity that neuters and spays feral cats in the San Fernando Valley in LA. The story of the Earth Cat Survivor is from the designer's imagination in which 'Astrokittys' are space explorers in search of planets that support feline life, but with the election of a 'petulant marmalade tabby' who is sceptical of climate change – funding has been cut. Enveloped in torched cedar wood shingles and lined with heat-pressed felt, these shelters are all that's left in Kowhow's imaginative world.

Name of Design: Germaine Name of Designers: Jessica Brancato and Antoine Guay	It looks like the chickens have come home to roost. Literally. With this indoor coop, these feathered friends can now have the same access to domestic indoor life as pet dogs and cats. It is formed of white coated steel, with metal mesh enveloping the trapezium-shaped structure. The door to the coop doubles as a ramp, leading to a raked ladder that offers entry to the sheltered sleeping quarters. The design promotes the inclusion of chickens in humans' daily life, and the project was included in *The Animal Party* exhibition at Geneva School of Art and Design, which examined the role of animals in our society.

Name of Design:
Cat Litter Box
Name of Company:
Chimère Edition

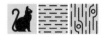

Resembling a sort of elegant spacecraft, this handcrafted litter box sits on two arched legs made of solid oak that support the oak base, with crossed aluminium bars adding bracing. The removable, smooth-edged top of the litter box makes for easy maintenance, with the lacquer shell available in white, grey or an aqua colour. When they discovered that it was hard to find beautiful pet furniture, creators of the Chimère Edition collection, Frédéric Stouls and designer Marc Ange, dedicated their lives to making pet furniture of exceptional quality and style, designed by Marc's creative studio: Bloom Room.

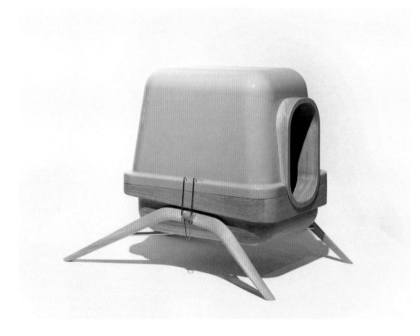

Name of Design:
Stables at El Mirador
Name of Company:
CC Arquitectos

Built in the middle of the woods, at the highest point of a hill south-west of Mexico City, sits El Pabellón El Mirador stables. The large, ground-floor entrance is designed to receive horse and rider, who enter a spacious and rustic area bound on three sides by reclaimed wooden railway sleepers that support the mezzanine. The water component of the concept extends outwards from the stable in the form of a reflective pool. This beautiful design changes with the seasons, as the natural chinks and cracks in the recycled wood encourage the growth of moss and plants, blending the structure into the natural surroundings.

Despite the 1994 hunting ban, thousands of bullets can still be found in the old hunting regions around Lebanon – with some from more recent illegal hunts. This stunning bird house is made from 2,500 stray brass bullets that were collected and welded piece by piece around the pear-shaped brass nest by local steel welders and craftsmen. Designer Makram el Kadi's design shows the paradox of life and death, hinting at the uncertainty of life during war. It was made for the Confessions 2012 collection organized by House of Today, a collaborative design platform who showcase Lebanese designers.

Name of Design:
Flora-Gato
Name of Company:
Formation Association

What appears to be a cross between an outdoor ottoman and a trellis sculpture is actually designed to house wild cats. The skeleton of the piece is made from recycled and fiberized plastic to create a lattice structure from which nature springs forth. Packed with Spanish moss and Korean grass, the interior of the shelter is shaded, with the temperature regulated by the evaporation of moisture – keeping the shelter comfortable for cats. This biomorphic structure was made in collaboration with Terremoto and Arktura as a contribution to the Giving Shelter charity event for FixNation, who work to spay and neuter feral cats.

Name of Design:
Copycat Art
Scratcher
Name of Designer:
Erik Stehmann

After an incident between an embroidered painting and his own cats, designer Erik Stehmann saw the funny side of cats tearing into a classic painting by one of the old masters, and it inspired him to create the Copycat Art Scratcher. Stehmann designed this fun product for cats and humans – whether it's Leonardo da Vinci's *Mona Lisa* or Johannes Vermeer's *Girl with the Pearl Earring*, the scratching posts are designed to be secured to the floor, or mounted on a wall. Made out of strong, durable sisal fibres, perfect for cats to scratch, the paintings are 70 x 50 centimetres (27.5 x 19.5 inches) in size.

With rising levels of unemployment during the recession, the drive to consume more locally produced food in a cost effective manner encouraged Wim and Bob Segers to design this self-sufficient chicken coop and vegetable garden. For the urban farmer, this unit can be located in residential areas, such as terraces or community gardens. The design features a long chicken run, and even a hutch for pet rabbits. A composting box processes kitchen waste, rainwater is collected for reuse, and there is storage for garden tools. Made out of thermally treated pinewood, the wood will age beautifully and slowly.

Name of Design:
Compact Cabinet
Name of Company:
Modernist Cat

Owner of Modernist Cat, Evan Gray Gregory endeavours to produce furniture that accommodates pets' needs and people's design expectations, to create a pet-friendly home. Handcrafted in Seattle, Washington, this modernist cabinet is made of a durable walnut-veneered plywood, treated with a water-resistant finish. The cabinet can be used as a cat cave, or even a discreet litter tray. There are entrances on both sides, to ventilate the interior – and allow for a quick getaway. The design allows for this Compact Cabinet to connect to the company's Standard Cabinet to form a large litter hideaway and pet house.

"Dogs are wise.
They crawl away into a quiet
corner and lick their wounds and
do not rejoin the world until they
are whole once more."

Agatha Christie

Name of Design:
Trench Cat
Name of Designers:
**Marc Eicher, Sarah
Bounab and Paul
Pourcelot**

Cat owners will know that when you give a cat a present, they want the box it came in, as they love to scratch it up. The Trench Cat could be one of the first mulitpurpose designs that takes advantage of this. This stylish jacket was designed for The Animal Party project by students at the Geneva School of Art and Design, and fills the gap in the market for items that cats can scratch, but look like they shouldn't. Fashioned on the traditional trench coat design, sisal fabric makes up the majority of the coat. By unbuttoning the fabric under the lapels, the sisal sleeves join together to form a snug bed.

Name of Design:
Bee Block & Bee Brick
Name of Company:
Green&Blue

The Green&Blue studio in Cornwall, UK, was set up in 2005 and has been creating beautiful products to aid wildlife ever since. With the decline of the wild bee population, the eventual impact on the environment will be devastating. These innovative and aesthetically pleasing designs by Gavin Christman seek to provide safe nesting places for solitary bees. Made from concrete in various colours, they can be built into a wall or left freestanding in a garden. Each cavity offers shelter and can be used to lay eggs in, with earth or vegetation sealing and protecting the entrance until they hatch in spring.

This bold design by architects Ma Yansong and Yosuke Hayano of MAD Architects breaks the mould of the traditional fishbowl. The purpose of this resin fish tank is to re-evaluate the human and fish relationship, by allowing the fish to dominate. The cubic tank appears to be deforming. Airways open up, these small channels seemingly lost in the mass of water, blurring the lines between where air and water begin, giving the effect of a larger and smoother interior for the fish. The erosion of the cubic space 'marks the end of the machine era', according to the designers, hinting at a more hopeful future for all.

Name of Design:
Rocking Birdcage
Name of Company:
Chimère Edition

Joining the elegant designs of the Chimère collection comes this rocking avian home. The joint venture by ex-banker Frédéric Stouls and designer Marc Ange, owner of Bloom Room design studio who created the birdcage for Chimère, aims to create timeless furniture by using the best materials, manufactured to the highest standards. See-sawing on solid oak rockers, the spherical cage is supported on aluminium legs that are counterbalanced by the weight of the oak-and-aluminium body. A small door is built into the surface of the cage, while a little perch hangs at the centre of this beautiful design.

Name of Design:
Holy Homes
Name of Company:
Frederik Roijé

'In my belief there will be peace' is the phrase that accompanies these two birdhouses with religious motifs designed by Frederik Roijé. Made from the finest porcelain, the Bird Mosque (right) is reminiscent of a traditional mosque, with its dome and minaret (or tower), along with its customary crescent moon symbol. The Bird Church (left), with its spear-like spire, vaulted ceiling and cross above the door, resembles a large cathedral. Both designs feature a unifying golden branch (or twig) made of glass, allowing a place for birds to perch, while providing easier access to the roost.

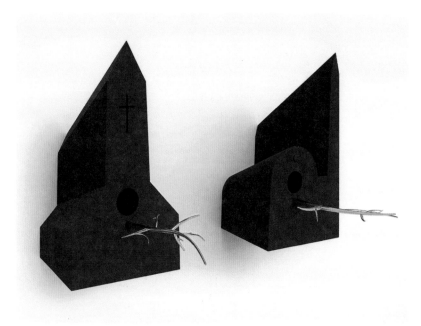

Running along Cardiff Bay in Wales, this striking 50 metre (164 foot) long wall contains 1,000 nest boxes for birds and bats. The wall was built to combat the shrinking natural habitat in the area, and to compensate for 1,000 newly built apartments nearby. Custom-made from Woodcrete (a combination of wood and concrete), there are four different sized houses to accommodate various flying creatures all year round. The wall acts not just as a home for these animals, but also acts as a divider between the private housing area and the pathway that runs along the public riverfront.

Name of Design:
**Leo Cat
Scratching Post**
Name of Company:
James Owen Design

This sleek cat scratching post is made from sustainable and durable mango wood mounted onto a brightly polished aluminium base. The bottom of this sturdy design is approximately 28 centimetres (11 inches) in diameter and has a slight curve, allowing the cat to knock it around, without it falling over. The grain of the mango wood is soft enough for the cat's claw sharpening but strong enough to be durable, with wear marks not visible due to the pattern and direction of the complex grain. The metal base and the wood scratching post can be separated to be recycled or replaced.

Name of Design:
**DOG Scratchpost
for Cats**
Name of Designer:
Erik Stehmann

From all the treats and the walks, to the 'who's a good boy?' praise, it's understandable that the historic rivalry between cats and dogs still lingers to this day. Just when it seems that dogs have it all, comes this playful cat scratcher in the shape of a dog. Treating design as toys for grown-ups, the ever-creative designer Erik Stehmann handmade the first DOG scratchpost as a joke for his cat Gerrit. But Gerrit didn't see it as a joke – he loved it. Modelled on a Labrador, the polyester base is wrapped in sisal rope, an extremely popular material for scratching, with every inch of rope glued by hand.

Name of Design:
Tunnel Home
Name of Company:
Full Loft

This multifunctional design works as an elevated dog bed as well as a side table. The integration of a pet bed with commonly used household furniture brings the dog closer into the folds of family life. The cube-shaped body is made of thermoformed poplar wood sheets that are held together via heat-treated steel brackets that surround the den, keeping the Tunnel Home supported and sturdy. On the top of the design are small hollows to accommodate electronic devices such as phones or tablets. Behind the large pillow for the dog to nap on is a cross-shaped opening that helps ventilate the kennel.

Name of Design:
Kläffer
Name of Company:
Nils Holger Moorman

From the Nils Holger Moorman furniture workshops in Aschau im Chiemgau, Germany, comes this wonderfully inventive dog-sized flat-pack bed. The pieces made by the designer Christoffer Martens and Mr Moorman himself are known for their intelligent, aesthetic and humorous designs, and this dog bed is no exception. Built of birch plywood components that interconnect without the need for screws or glue, this minimalist bed is simple to set up, and is extremely easy to deconstruct and move. Martens has even created adult and child-sized flat-pack beds, so that no one in the family feels left out.

Name of Design:
Spontaneous City in the Tree of Heaven
Name of Company:
London Fieldworks

Commissioned by local councils as part of the Secret Garden Project, London Fieldworks conceived this project in 2010. The design focused on two bird and insect homes, in two specific trees, on opposite sides of London. These wooden homes are constructed around the trees commonly known as 'the Tree of Heaven' (*ailanthus altissima*), and reference the architecture that surrounds them. The birds' nest and bug boxes in Duncan Terrace in Islington recall the surrounding Georgian terraces and 1960s housing estates, while over in Kensington and Chelsea, the design mirrors the nearby World's End housing estate.

Name of Design:
Mouldable Blanket
Name of Company:
DOTE

After a fruitless search for elegant, modern and sustainable products for their cats, Nic Wallenberg and Helena Hedenstedt decided to make their own. Comprising one hundred per cent recycled felt from the leftovers of other DOTE designs, each blanket has a unique pattern and colour. The blanket has superfine copper wire woven into the edge of the fabric, making the design malleable and able to be sculpted into a variety of shapes to suit the cat's temperament; for example, it can be moulded into a sheltered cave for the sleepy or introverted, or into tunnels for the extroverted and adventurous cat.

Name of Design:
Canal Bird House
Name of Company:
Frederik Roijé

Designed for the world-renowned Rijksmuseum, the canal bird house is a tribute to the Dutch Golden Age of the seventeenth century that saw trade, art and science flourish to such an extent that the country's influence spread around the world. These DIY bird house kits mimic the streetscapes of seventeenth century Amsterdam. The brass nails that hold the nests together represent the grandeur and opulence of the iconic buildings. Two types of canal bird house are available: the bell-shaped gable and the step-shaped gable, both crafted from black-painted, weatherproof plywood.

Name of Design:
MiaCara Covo
Name of Designer:
Uta Cossmann

The Covo dog basket was conceived to give pets the practical and comfortable bed they deserve, whilst being a beautiful object in its own right, just right for the design-conscious pet owner. The frame of the basket is made from bent plywood, which is especially strong and robust. It is raised at the back to create a protective, enclosed feeling to the bed, encouraging the dog to curl up and get cosy. The bed comes with a foam-filled cushion, providing support and comfort, and is available with a fabric or a faux-fur cover. The dog basket comes in two different wood finishes, walnut or oak.

Name of Design:
Breed Retreat
Name of Company:
Frederik Roijé

This architectural hen house designed by Frederik Roijé resulted from a hope that public parks like the Vondelpark in Amsterdam or Central Park in New York would one day have a Breed Retreat, to house their own 'city chickens'. Comprised of individual compartments that are combined together, the wooden structure is intended to represent the natural pecking order of chickens: 'the higher the nest, the more secure'. The structure's internal lighting is powered via solar panels built into the roof. It simulates the light of long summer days during the darker months of the year, allowing the chickens to lay eggs all year round.

Name of Design:
Tunnel
Name of Company:
Brando Design

This Cor-Ten steel 'tunnel for cats' can be adapted to suit all types of feline characters and can be situated indoors or out. For the cat that likes to be involved in the daily goings-on of family life, steel legs raise the tunnel off the ground, turning it into the perfect viewing platform, with the rectangular holes piercing the carapace – perfect for spying. Alternatively the Tunnel can be mounted to the wall in a discreet location for the more hesitant feline. Because cats prefers to feel secure while not being trapped, the piece is shaped like a tunnel, with the two diametrically opposed openings providing both entrance and exit.

Name of Design:
Loulie Cat Tower
Name of Company:
WOWBOW London

Cats don't ask for much. They want some attention, extremely luxurious surroundings, and complete world domination. This contemporary cat tower and bed ticks off at least two of these requirements. Elevated just under fifty centimetres (twenty inches) off the ground, the acrylic tower acts as a vantage point so that cats can keep tabs on their surroundings. Crowning the top of the design is a deluxe sheepskin cushion filled with memory foam. Even though WowBow's aim is to spoil pets with their designs, a percentage of all their sales goes towards animal welfare charities in the UK.

Name of Design:
Cubic Pulse 160
Jellyfish Tank
Name of Company:
Cubic Aquarium
Systems

This whopping jellyfish aquarium can hold 174 litres (38 gallons) of water. The largest tank in Cubic's range is designed for a considerable number of jellyfish. Built of one hundred per cent cast acrylic with a ten millimetre ($\frac{1}{2}$ inch) thick external frame, the aquarium comes in either black or white, with inbuilt colour changing LED lights that can be controlled remotely. Researched and developed by aquatic experts, the tank is suitable for numerous types of jellyfish, with a built-in mechanical and biological filtration system to keep the water at optimal levels and clear of algae.

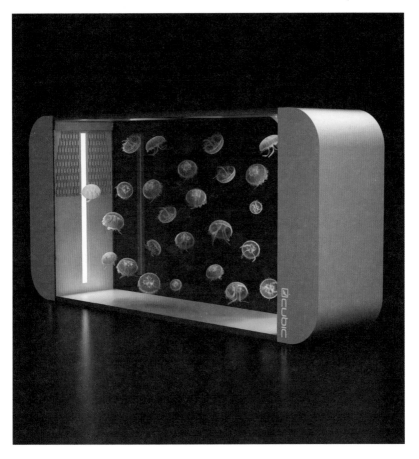

Bold, elegant and luxurious, the Dedalo is typical of high quality Italian design. Endeavouring to bring higher quality furniture for pets to the market, PetSuperfine use the best materials to form the most durable and aesthetic designs. Several cold bent steel strips slightly overlap to configure the spherical element of the design, with a bent wood insert encircling the bed and anchoring the metal sheets. The gaps in the overlapping metal create two large openings for a pet to enter, with a circular, stain-resistant microfibre cushion lining the base. It is supported by manually turned legs, available in a number of wood options.

Name of Design:
Kitty Ball Cat Bed
Name of Company:
The Refined Feline

Complementing any contemporary living space with this design made of natural materials, the Kitty Ball Cat Bed by The Refined Feline group offers an elegant and comfortable bed elevated off the ground yet easy to access – allowing the cat to lounge up high, keeping an eye on things. Handwoven from faux rattan with an espresso-colour finish, the material is non-toxic and extremely durable, as well as being advantageous for cats who like to scratch furniture. The 43 centimetre (17 inch) diameter dome is lined with a soft and washable cushion, perfect for the feline of the house.

Name of Design:
Built-in Dog Bed/Lin Residence
Name of Company:
LCGA Design

When LCGA Design began drawing up plans for this apartment, the owners asked them to include a designated space for their dog. Located next to the Tamsui River in Taiwan, this minimalist open-plan apartment features a built-in dog bed. Combining a divider screen, a side table and a dog bed, the metal and wood veneer structure forms a cosy custom-designed enclosure. Running alongside the sofa, the side table acts as the roof over the bed, which in turn merges with one of the shelves of the tall shelving – functioning primarily as a room divider – perfect for the open-plan design.

"Dogs have owners,
cats have staff."

Anonymous

Name of Design:
Cat Console
Name of Company:
Modernist Cat

'Made for pets, designed for you': the credo of all Modernist Cat products is evident in this imaginative piece. Both a console table and a cat scratcher, this design integrates the needs of the pet with the functions of human furniture, strengthening the pet-owner relationship. The table is handcrafted from thirteen layers of birch veneer, topped with a hardwood, walnut veneer. The two-legged slanting table has a narrow display shelf, under which there is an exposed storage shelf. The console attaches to a wall and features a colourful scratch pad that can be replaced when needed.

Name of Design:
The Cone
Name of Company:
Wiski

Wiski was born out of a desire to make cat furniture that would fit in with any contemporary interior – and be loved by cats. The Cone is a contemporary scratching post that also contains the perfect spot to nap within the elevated sleeping space, and was created especially for McCallister, the grey tabby owned by designer Evan Ryan. This fetching cone-shaped design is comprised of a steel frame and a one hundred per cent natural sisal cover which is adored by cats for its brilliant scratch appeal. The 80 centimetre ($31\frac{1}{2}$ inch) tall structure is sturdily supported on its 40 centimetre (16 inch) diameter base.

Name of Design:
**Acrylic White
Curved Bed**
Name of Company:
Pet Lounge Studios

White, bright and elegant, this minimalist bed references the popular designs of the 1950s and 60s. Made of acrylic, a desirable material for its malleability, strength and durability, the walls of the bed simply curve around the oval base with a small opening for accessibility. At 46 centimetres (18½ inches) wide and 22 centimetres (8½ inches) high, the bed was designed for a small dog. Pet Lounge Studios is made up of a group of passionate designers and animal lovers who frequently work with bamboo, due to its resourcefulness, its opulent appearance and sustainability as a source of material.

Name of Design:
Pet Bed
Name of Designer:
Seungji Mun

A part of the Pet Furniture Collection by Korean designer Seungji Mun, the range seeks to cater for the increasing number of people living alongside pets, with the research and designs focusing primarily on the needs of puppies. The bed is made of an eco-friendly waterproof cover that comes in a variety of colours, and can be removed and cleaned, making it ideal for toilet training. The antibacterial cover protects the soft sponge interior, which is more comfortable than cotton alternatives. The bed fits perfectly inside the Pet House (p.43) which is part of the same collection.

Name of Design:
The Ball
Name of Company:
Meyou Paris

Reflecting on how few designs for cats really measured up to their design expectations, Aude Sanchez and Vito Saccaro formed Meyou Paris to create refined furniture that would appeal to design-conscious pet owners as well as enhancing the comfort and life of cats. The centrepiece of this elegant design is the ball. Handwoven to form a beautiful cocoon that has an ideal texture for scratching, it houses an enclosed space for the cat's lair, with the circular entrance large enough to ventilate the interior. Supporting this sleeping module is the surrounding frame made of beech wood, which is braced with metal rods.

Name of Design:
**MiaCara Letto
dayBed**
Name of Designer:
Gerd Couckuyt

Abiding by the Modernist philosophy of 'form follows function', this range of pet products meets the requirements of durability and comfort, while remaining both stylish and modern. Designer Gerd Couckuyt conceived this daybed, inspired by nature: 'Curly leaves fall off the trees in the autumn, so I came up with the idea to work from a single plate and let this curl up along the edges in one smooth movement like those leaves.' The frame is powder-coated aluminium, the upturned sides defining the dog's own space, and is lined with a fabric-covered foam mattress, providing the perfect place to nap.

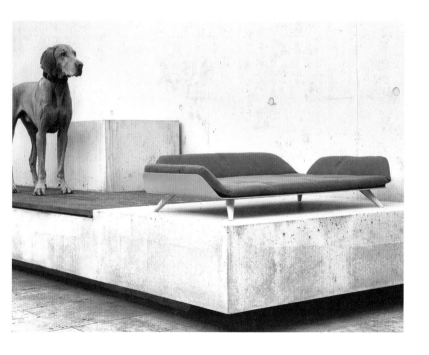

Name of Design:
Dog Cooler
Name of Designer:
Hiroshi Naito

Hiroshi Naito's contribution to Kenya Hara's Architecture for Dogs initiative was a tribute to his late dog, Pepe. He found that the fluffy Spitz would struggle during the humid Japanese summers, seeking to cool himself by lying on the bathroom tiles. In his memory, this design aims to lower the body temperature of overheating dogs. Using the thermally conductive properties of metal, the aluminium pipes can be filled with bags of ice. Wooden slats are positioned in between the tubes for the dog's claws to gain leverage, with a rubber hose connecting the metal to the wood in order to sculpt the design.

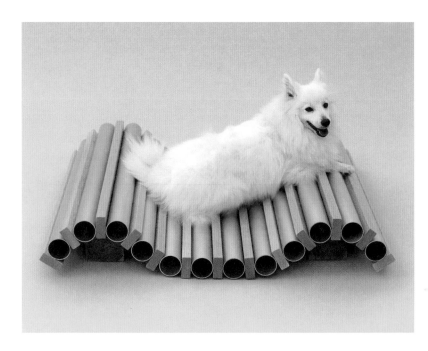

Name of Design:
BBung-a House
Name of Company:
POTE

South Korean design company POTE are the creators of this charming design. With a name that means 'best friend' or 'mate' in French, the company design items that create connections between humans and their trusted animal companions. Formed of numerous birch plywood slats that resemble fish bones, the hollowed interior space is the perfect safe place for a cat, or even a small dog. The slats are perfectly distanced from each other to provide sightlines from within, while allowing the pet to enjoy spending time with their owner from the comfort of their own safe space.

Name of Design:
Dwell Crate
Name of Company:
Modernist Cat

Designed and handcrafted in Seattle, Washington, this Mid-Century Modern-style dog crate gives space and comfort to the pet, while simultaneously functioning as a cabinet. The body of the crate, with its removable legs, is made of walnut-veneered plywood with a water-resistant finish. The dog bed can be turned into a crate to secure the pet by inserting the removable sliding door into the opening above the entrance, which can be stowed in the rear compartment when not in use. Rectangular openings in the sides, offer light and ventilation to the interior, which is lined with a fleece-covered bed.

Name of Design:
Reading Cat
Name of Company:
Wohnblock

This sophisticated design by Oliver Kriege for Wohnblock works not only as a book shelf and room divider, but also as a cat's domain from which to rule. Standing just less than 1.8 metres (6 feet) tall, the summit of the wooden structure is made accessible by seven of the shelves that extend out from the rear of the tower to create a cat-accessible ladder. Each block is adorned with a durable carpet and a scratching board. The multi-levelled rectangular platforms come in variations titled the 'Sleeping platform', the 'Resting bench' and the 'Lounging perch'. All suitably named for the cat that prefers the quiet life.

Name of Design:
Pet Camper
Name of Company:
Straight Line Designs

Dogs have long been denied the joys of getting away from it all in a campervan. Cost-effective and manoeuvrable, the benefits of having a campervan are – it is claimed – endless. And now, thanks to Judson Beaumont of Straight Line Designs based in Vancouver, Canada, custom-built mini campers allow dogs to share the joy. Reminiscent of the classic American Airstream trailer, this metal design is just 35 centimetres (14 inches) wide, 89 centimetres (35 inches) long, 50 centimetres (19½ inches) high, and weighs only 11 kilograms (25 pounds). Each handmade camper comes with a personalized number plate.

Name of Design:
Gimli Traveller Den
Name of Company:
Gamla Studio

Created for the designer's Welsh terrier (called Gimli), is this multipurpose dog den and carrier, created for pets – and their owners – to travel in style. Encasing the den is a powder-coated aluminium mesh wall that lets in plenty of light, keeping the dog safe without the size and bulk of a regular cage. The lightweight frame is made of beautiful, sustainably harvested black walnut wood, with a non-toxic and one hundred per cent natural finish that keeps the dog away from harmful chemicals. Accents include solid brass fittings and leather, making this a safe and comforting space for a dog.

Friends and designers Maud Beauchamp and Marie-Pier Guilmain formed their company Loyal Luxe in order to make fun, stylish, affordable and eco-friendly designs. Constructed from 87 per cent recycled corrugated cardboard, this flat-packed teepee can be assembled in two minutes without the need for glue or tools. The teepee is ideal for cardboard box-loving cats, and features six attachable and exchangeable ornaments, including a dream catcher, a bull's head, a feather, an eagle, a tomahawk and a placard to write either the cat's name or perhaps 'Dogs Not Allowed'.

This exciting piece of furniture designed by Studio PAULBAUT is a cross between the archetypal rocking chair and a pet bed. The design was envisaged via 3D modelling, with various small prototypes made by 3D printing. These were used to refine the balance and design, followed by the chair being manufactured by CNC milling (computer-controlled cutting). Combining a shelter for cats or dogs with the relaxing rocking nature of the chair creates a personal bond between pet and owner when reclining. The CNC-milled ribs are made of birch plywood with a clear coat finish.

Name of Design:
Catissa Geobed
Name of Company:
Catissa

The Catissa Geobed, by Russian designer Ilshat Garipov of Catissa, is a multi-faceted pet bed that is designed for cats and small dogs. The triangular pieces that form the bed are attached to one another by wooden pegs, with a break in the attaching triangles allowing the pet to get in and out of this cave-like home, and providing the cat or dog with their own area to relax in. Made of natural birch plywood and finished with a water-based varnish, the bed is available in natural wood, white and black options, with a sheepskin or faux-fur cushion lining the bottom of the bed. Ilshat's design won the Design&Design Award in 2015.

Name of Design:
Nidin
Name of Company:
Fabbricabois

Inspired by the Japanese art of origami, this multipurpose design by Fabbricabois is supported without the use of screws or glue. Six pieces of birch plywood are cut and assembled to form a beautiful design that functions as a coffee table, pet shelter and magazine rack. Two large elastic straps hold the rectangular, triangular and square pieces of birch plywood together, with angled incisions on the floor and on the table top to support the walls of the animal shelter and magazine rack. The design is perfect for the dog that wants to be in the centre of a living area or close to its owner.

Name of Design:
**Modern Cat Tree
NEKO**
Name of Company:
Rinn

Wondering whether it was possible to create practical cat furniture in a contemporary style, designer Yoh Komiyama crafted this inspired piece. The base is made of natural marble, an unconventional material for pets, but perfect for minimal interiors and stabilising the cat tree. Hemp cord is wrapped around the main pillar to create a scratching post, with circular Japanese hardwood slats enclosing the design and allowing pet and owner to remain in contact. The structure can be opened via a hinged panel, revealing three climbable platforms lined in Danish Kvadrat fabric.

211

"There is nothing in which the birds differ more from man than the way in which they can build and yet leave a landscape as it was before."

Robert Lynd

This playful one square metre (ten square foot) feline structure is made from acrylic sheet, timber panels and artificial grass. Designer Jessica Ginther of HOK Architects created this multi-level cat house for the inaugural Giving Shelter benefit held by Architects for Animals – helping raise funds for the Los Angeles–based charity FixNation, which works to neuter and spay homeless cats. The simple design caters for numerous cats – all within a Jenga-like structure that supports four gable-roofed houses. These in turn support a larger timber gable, with artificial turf completing the design.

Name of Design:
Catwheel II
Name of Company:
Catswall Design

Set on a secure base, the revolving 120 centimetre (47 inch) diameter wheel is designed to work as a treadmill for cats, in addition to being a stand-alone piece of indoor sculpture. The PVC fabric track allows cats to jump in from both sides, and is stable enough for fast-running felines. The material is perfect for grip and wide enough to allow for three cats to run abreast, with the additional rollers in the base designed to be silent when the wheel is in motion. The Catwheel II is perfect for small living spaces and complements any style of interior design – as well as improving the physical health of the cat.

Name of Design:
Cat House Berta
Name of Company:
Pet-interiors

After a long time hunting for an elegant and suitable house for their beloved cat Mrs Schmitt, the owners hit a dead end. Nothing was suitable. This was the catalyst for what would become Pet-interiors, a product design company that locates craftspeople to realize their pet-friendly designs. This cave-like pod is almost entirely enclosed, and consists entirely of one hundred per cent natural wool felt, making it an ideal retreat for the cat or kitten that is sensitive to noise, due to the material's ability to absorb sound. Indeed, the only sound likely to be heard will be a purr of contentment from within this retreat.

Name of Design:
Cat in the Fish Bowl
Name of Company:
**Abramson Teiger
Architects**

The Managing Principal at Abramson Teiger Architects, Douglas Teiger, has always believed that architecture has the power to raise people's souls to a higher spiritual level. Created for Los Angeles charity FixNation's fundraiser, it was inspired by the yin-yang symbol that represents complementary (rather than opposing) forces that interact to form a dynamic system in which the whole is greater than the assembled parts. A series of wooden layers form the irregular-shaped bowl, leaving the cat free to explore and play. Doubling as a side table, the multifunctional design is topped with playful green turf.

Name of Design:
Silhouette
Name of Company:
CallisonRTKL

Made for the annual Giving Shelter initiative that aims to raise money for FixNation, a non-profit organization that works to neuter and spay feral cats in Los Angeles, comes this exciting design. Composed of undulating wooden slats, this impressive structure was inspired by the geometry of ancient cathedrals, known for their incredible size. A carpeted ramp runs from the rear of the design to a raised perch that cats can observe from, while maintaining cover. The vaulted interior is perfect to escape the elements, with several smaller arches acting as entrances for cats that don't want to make a fuss.

Name of Design:
Kitty Condo
Name of Company:
Stantec

Stantec's response to the Architects for Animals Giving Shelter initiative was Kitty Condo – one of thirteen designs aimed to raise funds for non-profit FixNation, which works to spay and neuter feral cats in the San Fernando Valley. Combining open artificial grass areas with hidden areas in the wooden structure, this open-air shelter aims to provide a high vantage point for curious cats and a place to lie in the sun, while also catering for shy feral cats. Twenty-three parallel timber slats form the walls, with breaks in the edifice for artificial lawns, making this structure resemble a block of residential apartments.

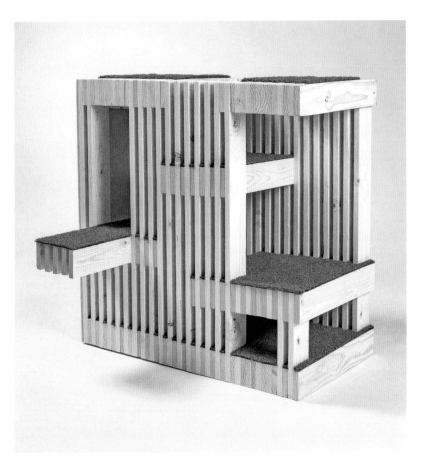

Name of Design:
HEX Tennis Dog Bed
Name of Designer:
Hugh Hayden

Up until now, dogs could only dream of reclining on a bed made of tennis balls, but this playful design in the HEX Tennis Furniture Collection by designer and artist Hugh Hayden has changed all that. The Brooklyn-based designer crafted the bed using more than a hundred recycled tennis balls that are tightly woven together into a hexagonal shape. The top row of balls defines the napping area and can hold a two-sided cushion that comes in black or red. The bed weighs only 11 kilograms (25 pounds) and is 66 centimetres (26 inches) in diameter, making it suitable for smaller dog breeds, but will be loved by all dogs.

Name of Design:
NekoPod
Name of Company:
Blink Pet

Blink Pet produced the NekoPod in a bid to create luxury housing for cats. By imagining how the world looks through a cat's eyes, the designers built the house to provide shelter for outdoor cats. The pod is made out of recycled plastic, and is composed of two attachable components. The top half's overhanging canopy shelters the main entrance from rain, keeping the interior dry. Stainless steel legs elevate the NekoPod, making sure heat is not lost through the ground. A unique one-way hatch at the back allows for cats to make a quick getaway – adding to the sense of security in this cat cocoon.

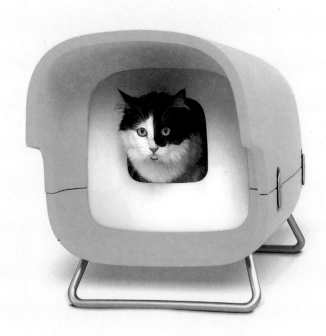

Name of Design:
LURVIG Play Tunnel
Name of Company:
IKEA

IKEA's LURVIG range by Inma Bermudéz includes a variety of simple, playful and affordable designs that focused on two elements when being made: the design from a pet's perspective, and matching human design with pet design. This extendable tunnel is aimed at the cat who likes to hide and seek, with four openings, and a playful ball attached to the tunnel's opening. The tunnel can connect to the LURVIG cat house, creating a long runway and an additional place for the cat to conceal themselves. The metal frame of the 128 centimetre (50 inch) tunnel can be retracted and stored away.

Name of Design:
Billy Plug
Name of Designers:
**Mathilde Porté and
Victor Prieux**

This inspired design came from two young students the Geneva School of Art and Design for a project directed by Alexandra Midal, titled 'The Animal Party'. Completed in a series of workshops at the school, this steel plate rodent cage clips on to the renowned IKEA Billy bookcase. Painted in a beautiful turquoise, the cage, comprised of hexagonal-shaped components seems to simply float off the shelves, with the bars creating a playful 3D illusion while also providing the rodents with their own climbing frame. Simple platforms run through the cage supporting the structure and create areas for the pets to explore.

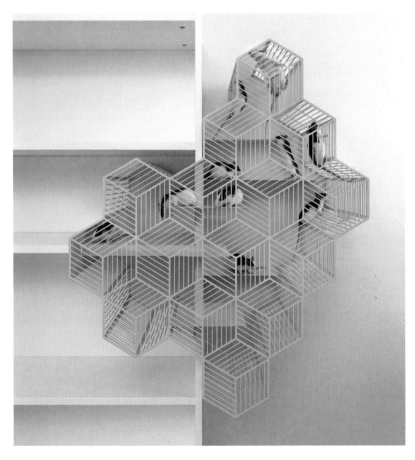

Name of Design:
Mount Pug
Name of Designer:
Kengo Kuma

Resembling a small mountain, Mount Pug is one of the thirteen designs for Architecture for Dogs – the exciting initiative led by the Hara Design Institute and Nippon Design Centre that commissioned renowned designers and architects to create dog-inspired architecture. Consisting of 74 branches of plywood, this impressive mound is completely self-supporting, with interlocking panels linked together to create the wooden mesh, using no glue or nails. At 800 millimetres (31.5 inches) high, this structure acts as shelter for the pug to play or sleep under. The multitude of openings allow for toys and treats to hang from Mount Pug.

Name of Design:
Caballeriza la Solana
Name of Company:
Nicolas Pinto da Mota

Located on a horse farm in Soriano, in western Uruguay, this stable is designed for the breeding and rearing of Criollo horses, a native breed of the area. The idea comes from a combination of practical aspects required of a stable, with a neutral and free-flowing design concept that works with the land and the needs of the horses. A steel roof protects the building, which holds eight stalls for the horses, and perforated concrete walls let in light. The stalls open on to the paddock outside via the individual exposed wooden doors – along with the sliding front door, which has been designed to weather beautifully with age.

Name of Design:
Larvik Dog House
Name of Company:
Bad Marlon

The designers from Bad Marlon seek to create a same-design –identity in which owner and pet coexist in harmony with one another, sharing experiences and feelings. This striking dog house is reminiscent of a tall building seen across a contemporary city skyline. The den consists of powder-coated steel on the sides, and plywood boards for the facade and back. Rectangular openings of differing sizes have been cut out of the walls and ceiling to allow in light and encourage airflow. This stylish piece fits in perfectly with the minimalist Black Frame Fence (p.99), also designed by Bad Marlon.

Name of Design:
Stork Nest Farm
Name of Company:
SGL Projekt

There is a lot to like about a horse-riding arena that resembles an enormous bird's nest. This stunning piece of architecture in the Czech Republic drew its inspiration from the storks that used to make nests in the chimney of the disused distillery on which the arena was built. With the stork as their symbol, the architects created this nest-like circular riding arena clad in over 200 tonnes (220 tons) of oak logs. Measuring 34 metres (111 feet) in diameter and 15½ metres (51 feet) high, the impressive exterior provides shading for the interior, with the skylight providing natural airflow and further regulating the temperature.

Name of Design:
Bat Cloud
Name of Company:
Ants of the Prairie

Hanging from the trees like gargantuan bats, these suspended vessels provide habitation for these winged mammals. With openings on all sides, the Bat Cloud encourages the bats to fly in and take residence in the upper part of the vessel. The base of each Bat Cloud holds soil and native plants, drawing other wildlife in, including a bat's preferred food: insects. This brilliant design is self-maintaining with the vegetation being fertilized by the guano (or bat droppings) that falls into the soil at the base of the vessel, underneath which, stainless steel mesh works as a drainage system.

Name of Design:
Kangaroo Enclosure
Name of Company:
White Arkitekter

If you have been struggling to find suitable housing for your Tasmanian kangaroo, look no further. Swedish architecture firm White Arkitekter designed this kangaroo enclosure for Copenhagen Zoo in order to bring humans closer to these wonderful animals. Thermal timber slats cloak the facade, with green sedum lining the roof and a heated floor made of concrete to keep the roos warm during cold weather. In order to respect their habitat and give them privacy, the enclosure is subdivided into segments, with the timber doors opening on to the animal-only field, allowing the kangaroos to meet visitors on their own terms.

Name of Design:
Bird Apartment
Name of Company:
Nendo

In the mountains of Nagano Prefecture in Japan, nestled among the trees in the Komoro City forest, resides Nendo's Bird Apartment. Designed for the Ando Momofuku Centre, the house was created to view nature. A section for bird homes and a space for humans divide the tree house. Seventy-eight gable-roofed bird nests form one end of the structure, with a wooden ladder leading up to the human-sized bird house. Numerous peepholes are located throughout the partition, allowing the nests to be viewed from the apartment. The light-painted timber panels are unobtrusive, blending the apartment into the natural environment.

Unable to find a stylish waterer and feeder for chickens, the Nottoscale team designed the Moop Bird Feeder. It is designed to feed three to four chickens with enough food or water to last up to five days. The hole at the top makes it easy to replenish the feed, filling up the bowl via three large openings, distributing it evenly. Made from glazed cream-coloured stoneware, the feeder is durable and easy to clean. It was designed to accompany the Moop (p.157), a modular chicken coop designed for an urban garden. The feeder is supported by nylon hangers that come in a variety of colours.

Name of Design:
Nestbox
Name of Company:
JAM Furniture

Welsh company JAM Furniture set out to make an eco-friendly nest for wild birds, resulting in the playful Nestbox, which is primarily made from recycled materials sourced from local manufacturers. The body of the design is made of fixed metal sheets from disused dishwashers and washing machines, while spare wooden parts from local businesses form the front and back of the nest. Once painted, the Nestbox can be placed on a tree for use by a variety of birds (the entry holes can be cut to four different sizes), with the textured brass perch providing grip for birds entering the roost.

"The Cat. He walked by himself,
and all places were alike to him."

Rudyard Kipling

Name of Design:
Cromo
Name of Company:
FORMA Italia

This striking outdoor doghouse is made of 13 millimetre ($\frac{1}{2}$ inch) thick plastic that grants great protection and insulation from poor weather. The house sits on four feet, and one ramp, made of varnished aluminium. Natural lighting is provided by a coloured translucent pane on the roof and ventilation is catered for via a grille made of the same durable plastic. The Cromo, with its minimalist white base and blue highlights, is also produced with a blue base and red highlights. The range comes from the new FORMA Italia branch of Chiavari, a new brand that solely focuses on luxury design for pets.

Name of Design:
Cat's Cradle
Name of Company:
DSH Architecture

This visually impressive design was created in 2014 for the Giving Shelter initiative, the Architects for Animals' benefit to raise money for the Los Angeles–based charity FixNation, which works to neuter and spay homeless cats in the San Fernando Valley. Five aluminium hoops are held together with rope – much loved by cats – resulting in this exciting structure. Three of the hoops act as the gravitational anchor of the design, forming the main part of the structure, while the 'key ring' and 'cat ring', wrapped in blue cord, double as a play space and a shelter from the hot Californian sun.

Name of Design:
Felt Cat Cave
Name of Company:
AgnesFelt

Having been raised by a mother and a grandmother who loved to knit and sew, and a great aunt who sheared sheep and had a spinning-wheel, it is unsurprising that Agnė Audėjienė has ended up making her living out of something to do with wool. Based in her homeland of Lithuania, she and her husband Robertas craft a variety of designs, specifically using heat-pressed felt, including this cat-eared cat cave. These made-to-order beds are handmade, using a variety of coloured wool. The small entrance hole at the front provides shelter, allowing cats to get away from it all.

241

Name of Design:
**Duplex Bird-
cage-aquarium**
Name of Company:
**Constance Guisset
Studio**

The Constance Guisset Studio aims to create work that is thought-provoking and allows 'a moment to escape in a dream'. This beautiful design certainly does that, proposing as it does, the co-habitation of two animals completely alien to one another. Fluttering within the steel cage beneath, the bird lives like any other pet bird does. However, a thermo-formed, bell-shaped air bubble above allows the bird to perch in the midst of a fish's world, separated only by glass. This unique birdcage-aquarium stands at 1 ½ metres (62 inches) high, and encourages the idea that species who live in different elements can live together.

Name of Design:
ConCATenate
Name of Company:
Lehrer Architects

Raising funds for FixNation, Architects for Animals' Giving Shelter initiative called for leading architects to design shelters for cats, resulting in Lehrer's ConCATenate. A series of ramps were welded together to form this ascending, multi-level feline play area. The layout encourages the cats to climb the right-angled shelving from the bottom up. Sixteen-gauge metal sheets form the structure, the white bands defining the pathways, while the three platforms available for the cats to play or sleep on are made of a playful blue artificial grass. The open design provides ventilation, but also shelter from the hot Los Angeles sun.

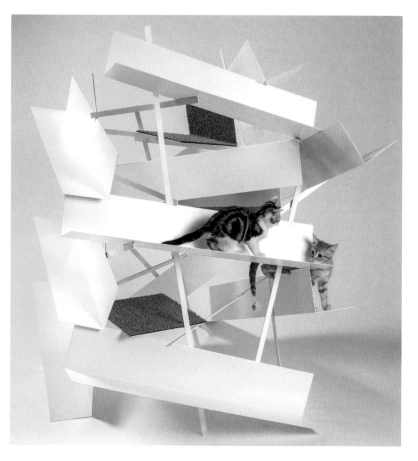

Name of Design:
Bird House
Name of Company:
Atelier Suburban

Using layers of birch plywood to form this charming egg-shaped bird's nest, the design allows rainwater to run off the surface. Finished in natural oil to protect the house, the simple design harmonizes and blends with nature. Depending on the birds seeking shelter, the Bird House comes in a large or a small size, the largest being 27 centimetres (11 inches) high and 19 centimetres (7 inches) wide, with a small 5 centimetres (2 inch) hole made for the entrance to the roost. The creators Irina Dragomir and Bogdan Ispas of Atelier Suburban in Bucharest, Romania, custom make all their wares, specializing in the use of wood.

Name of Design:
UnFURled
Name of Company:
Perkins+Will

This rollercoaster for cats consists of wooden trelliswork lined with turquoise felt. Assembled from detachable pieces, this cat architecture is designed to suit a multitude of different environments, the curving lattice ramps combining to create numerous loop-the-loops. Fun not only for the cat, this malleable design becomes an interactive play area, an object to deepen the bond between the pet and owner. UnFURled was built in honour of Architects for Animals' Giving Shelter fundraiser for FixNation, a non-profit organization that runs a full-time neuter and spay clinic for feral cats in the heart of the San Fernando Valley.

Name of Design:
Beagle House
Name of Company:
MVRDV

Created with the good-natured and playful characteristics of the beagle in mind, the Beagle House was a design commissioned by the Hara Design Institute and Nippon Design Centre for Design Miami 2012. Looking to create an interactive space for the beagle to sleep and play, the designers MVRDV took the archetypal notion of a dog house and made the floor, walls and roof gently bow upwards, creating a curve that causes the house to rock gently. This canine equivalent of a rocking chair is entirely made of wood and weighs just five kilograms (11 pounds), making this home lightweight and portable.

Name of Design:
Stairs For Dogs
Name of Company:
07BEACH

The method for designing this house in Ho Chi Minh City, Vietnam, was relatively simple. It was built to be a comfortable space for the residents, with surroundings that reflect the various personalities within the family. Architect Joe Chikamori discovered that the family loved their pets and requested that the stairs be made a suitable size and incline for their small dogs. This was the starting point for the built-in stairs. Why not have both? With a handrail for both owner and dog, the half-sized stairs run alongside the normal staircase, and extend around the wall of the bottom floor, enabling pet and owner to climb together.

Handmade in the Czech Republic by designer Boleslav Daška of design studio Dilna Hammer, these colourful wooden modules are designed specifically to house wild bees. The hexagonal hotels are reminiscent of natural honeycomb, providing a home for solitary bees, bumblebees and even ladybugs. Stuffed with bamboo shoots and pieces of wood, the bees can crawl into various nooks and crannies to hide in the summer, and hibernate in the winter. Simple yet elegant designs like this man-made home for bees not only sustain and increase the bee population, but bring life to surrounding gardens.

Name of Design:
Attic
Name of Company:
Studio Chad Wright

Tearing up the conventional bird house, Chad Wright's towering wooden nesting boxes seem to come straight out of an animated film. Wanting to bring the bird house to the bird, these avian homes rocket into the sky. Differing in height from 1.4 metres (4½ feet) to 1.8 metres (6 feet) tall, these slender homes accommodate a variety of birds all year round, and can be fixed into position with the stake screwed into its concrete base. These brightly coloured nests come in tomato red, robin's egg blue and cloud white. With an overhanging roof, small dowel perch and a faux chimney, these nests are quite the stylish bird home.

Name of Design:
Figueras Polo Stables
Name of Company:
Estudio Ramos

Standing next to a polo field on the vast plains of La Pampa in Argentina, these stables were commissioned by champion polo player, Nacho Figueras. The complex covers 3,850 square metres (41,441 square feet) and incorporates 44 stalls, a tack room, a roof terrace and a huge pond. The stables are primarily constructed from exposed concrete and local hardwoods. A bold and overtly modern structure, it displays a clarity of line and a pronounced horizontal aesthetic that allows it to complement the surrounding landscape – a harmonious relationship enhanced by the indigenous wild grasses planted on the roof.

Name of Design:
Exo
Name of Designer:
Evan McDougall

This wonderful tree-mounted bird house was purpose-built in order to help black-capped chickadees survive the harsh Canadian winters. A non-migratory bird that often has to survive up to -40°C (also -40°F) winters in the Arctic region of North America, the chickadee survives by being able to store thousands of seeds for rationing during the colder months. The Exo is made of cedar wood, the oils of which are moisture-resistant. Durable rubber envelopes the design to add to the insulation while also providing numerous openings to the grooves running along the wood, which can hold an abundance of seeds.

Name of Design:
Birdball Belle Feeder
Name of Company:
Green&Blue

The beautiful bird feeders by Green&Blue are made to withstand all types of weather all year round. Slipcast in clay, the small 9 centimetres ($3\frac{1}{2}$ inch) diameter feeder has a lovely glossy finish and is available is numerous pastel colours. Cradling the ball is a metal spiral that just hugs the lip of the ceramic, allowing the birds to grip on and feed. The design is perfect for smaller birds such as tits, sparrows, nuthatches and finches to feed, or even obtain nesting material by placing clumps of wool in the Birdball. A stainless steel wire supports the feeder, which is suspended from a sleeve to protect the tree it hangs from.

These two magnificent beehives stand on a rooftop in Oslo. The project was designed by Norwegian architecture studio Snøhetta, in response to the global decline of honeybee colonies. These urban beehives act as a source of bespoke honey that is sold below in the Mathallen Food Court, as well as raising public awareness to the plight of bees. Made from honey-coloured timber, the structure is formed by two intersecting hexagonal volumes, to create large honeycombs, with a honeycomb-like pattern covering the external surface. A small lip is cut near the base of the hive, providing bees with access to the hive.

Name of Design:
K-abeilles
Name of Company:
AJEANCE

Resembling a large hive that accommodates both humans and insects, the honeycomb-patterned K-abeilles is constructed entirely from wood. The facade is made of hexagonal microhabitats, drawing wild insects into the structure with numerous nooks and crannies made of wood, brick, hay and other materials. The arresting design is not only a hotel for bees; on the other side it offers a refuge for humans. The wooden planks in the interior form seats that allow people to sit and observe the insects, encouraging two very different species to socialise. The open cells provide views of the surrounding landscape.

This petting zoo in Öhringen, Germany (which also incorporates an aviary) was designed by Kresings Architektur and stands in an urban parkland setting. In addition to pitching the buildings at heights and angles suitable for the eye-level of the most important visitors – children – they also, in consultation with veterinary practitioners, employed larch for the primarily wooden and highly distinctive ribbed structures. Extremely durable, larch, unlike most other timbers when employed externally and left exposed, doesn't require chemical treatment against rot or infestation which is so often toxic to animals.

"I've seen a look in dogs' eyes,
a quickly vanishing look of amazed
contempt, and I am convinced
that basically dogs think
humans are nuts."

John Steinbeck

Name of Design:
Waterscape
Name of Designer:
Haruka Misawa

This stunning selection of minimalist aquariums is a part of the Waterscape collection. What started out as an experiment led to the discovery that beautiful, intricate designs that would normally collapse under their own weight out of water, are possible to achieve with the buoyancy of the water supporting the designs. Each of these translucent cube fishbowls holds a unique interior. With the use of 3D printing, complex designs are made possible, with small pathways for the fish to navigate through. Even more impressive are the bubble-like structures that house their own aquatic plant life, creating an ecosystem within an ecosystem.

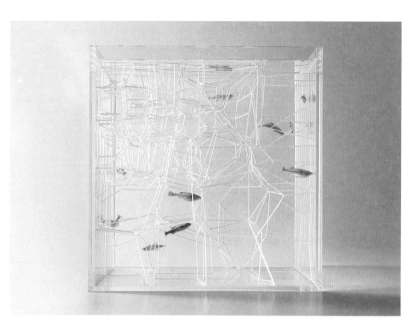

Name of Design:
Cat Tunnel Sofa
Name of Designer:
Seungji Mun

Designer Seungji Mun worked in collaboration with Yongjeh Park and Kangkyoung Lee to create this playful design for his Pet House Collection. With more than ten million individuals owning pets in Korea, there has been a shift in attitudes towards animal ownership, with the pet becoming a member of the family. By manipulating conventional furniture such as the sofa into a cat's play-and-rest area, the furniture is used as a tool to share experiences and emotions with an animal companion. Tapping into a cat's disposition for discovery and play, the built-in fabric lined tunnels are designed for the curious cat.

Name of Design:
Concrete Dog House
Name of Designer:
Tina Rugelj

This playful dog house comes from the Concrete Garden range – a line of outdoor furniture made entirely of concrete that is designed to live outside all year round. Slovenian architect and interior designer Tina Rugelj created the pieces out of natural fibre cement, a marvellous material chosen for its durability and its easy impact on the environment (consisting of 95 per cent natural materials including cement, pulverized limestone, air and water). One of the thinnest concretes available, not only is it lightweight and weather-resistant, minor imperfections along its surface lend a unique patina as it weathers and ages.

Name of Design:
LURVIG Pet Bed
Name of Company:
IKEA

Inma Bermudéz, the designer of the LURVIG pet range, has extended the joys of IKEA to all pets around the world – without them having to assemble any flat-packed furniture. The 62-piece range is for both cats and dogs, with the designs helping them to travel, eat, sleep and play. This joyful reworking of the classic IKEA sofa bed is made of polyester, with a polyurethane foam filling. The cushioned seat folds forward to form a bed for an extended sleeping area. At just 30 centimetres (11½ inches) tall, and 68 centimetres (26½ inches) wide, this compact bed is designed to complement any interior.

Name of Design:
LURVIG Cat House
Name of Company:
IKEA

The innovative and playful LURVIG range by designer Inma Bermudéz is specifically designed for pets. This multifunctional house for cats can detach from the rubber-bottomed legs to be mounted on a wall or even slide into IKEA's KALLAX shelf unit; additionally, it can work as a nightstand next to a bed. The entrance to the house is covered by a half-door or 'scratching wall' where a cat can sharpen its claws, leading to an enclosed space lined with a fitted cushion in green. The LURVIG play tunnel for cats (p.223) can be linked to the entrance to form a playful pathway to the cat's shelter.

Name of Design:
Apiarium Hive
Name of Designer:
Bettina Madita Böhm

The basic hive component of the Apiarum system is comprised of a cylindrical concrete module – a shape inspired by the bee's natural habitat, a hollow tree. As the bees form the honeycomb, an additional concrete chamber is added with hexagonal wooden frames that can be removed to harvest the honey. The lightweight concrete incorporates small air canals that keep the interior cool during hotter months, and can be filled with straw for warmth during the winter, while a flowerpot at the top attracts the bees. The hive is a means of encouraging city-dwellers to help increase the world's rapidly declining bee population.

The innovative designers at Nendo create products that question the accepted aesthetic of everyday objects. For example, many traditional products made for dogs are, according to Nendo, 'rounded and cutesy'. In contrast, their Cubic Pet Goods range reimagined these conventional stereotypes. A square toy, a house, a food bowl and a ball make up the collection, with the fabric dog house comprising two parts: a zip connects the upper and lower sections, depending on the dog's preference for a bed or a shelter; alternatively, the dog can just flop down on top of it, making one big squashed bed.

Name of Design:
Reflection
Name of Designer:
Andrew Loh

Designed as a part of The Missing Dining Table collection that appeared at Milan Design Week in 2016, this selection of work looks at the way we dine and offers inspiration for the possible dining habits of the future. Wanting to bring pet and owner closer together with synchronized eating times, the table is fitted with a sensor that triggers the food dispenser, and video relay from the camera when a plate of food is laid on the surface, allowing owner and pet to dine face-to-face. The table is made of plywood and white laminate, with copper rod railings defining the solitary table.

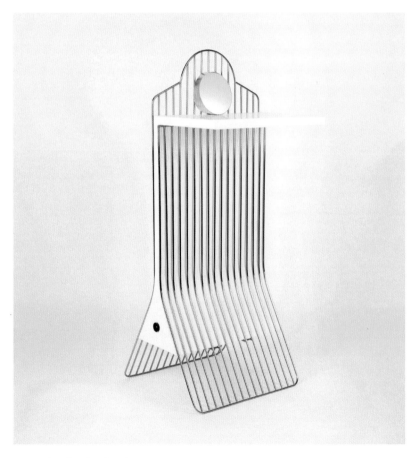

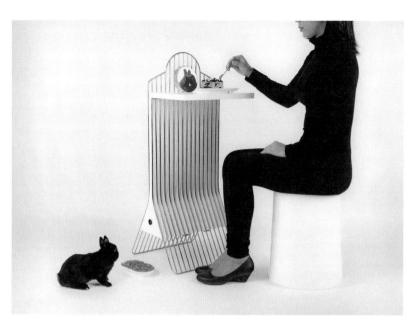

271

This elegant bird feeder works on the principle that a bird companion, or 'sidekick', should be able to eat their meal alongside human diners. The circular copper base acts as the foundation for the six metal poles that create this elevated bird table. Four copper pillars rise on their own to hold the ceramic bowls that hold seeds, fruit, millet and water. The other poles make up the budgerigar's perch, bringing her to the perfect height. The design was the invention of first-year student Jessica Dubochet for *The Animal Party* exhibition, led by Alexandra Midal at the Geneva School of Art and Design .

The Animal Party exhibition, an exciting project led by Alexandra Midal, sees a variety of work from the students at the Geneva School of Art and Design, exploring the role of pets and animals in our society. The second-year students Charlyne Boulet and Virginie Taché came up with the inventive idea of being able to turn any vase into a working aquarium. The arboreal design is made of durable Corian, and seems to branch out of the vase. The beautiful coral-like scrolls conceal the discreet water filter to the aquarium, and the overhanging offshoots are designed to be a handy key holder.

Where To Buy

Pet Directory

Index

Where to Buy

Directory of Pets

Bats

Birds

Cats

Page numbers in *italics* refer
to illustrations

Picture credits

Phaidon Press Limited
Regent's Wharf
All Saints Street
London N1 9PA

Phaidon Press Inc.
65 Bleecker Street
New York, NY 10012

phaidon.com

First published 2018
© 2018 Phaidon Press Limited

ISBN 978 0 7148 7667 2

Commissioning Editor: Virginia McLeod
Project Editor: Tom Wainwright
Picture Research: Tom Wainwright
Production Controller: Sarah Kramer

Design: StudioKanna

Printed in Hong Kong

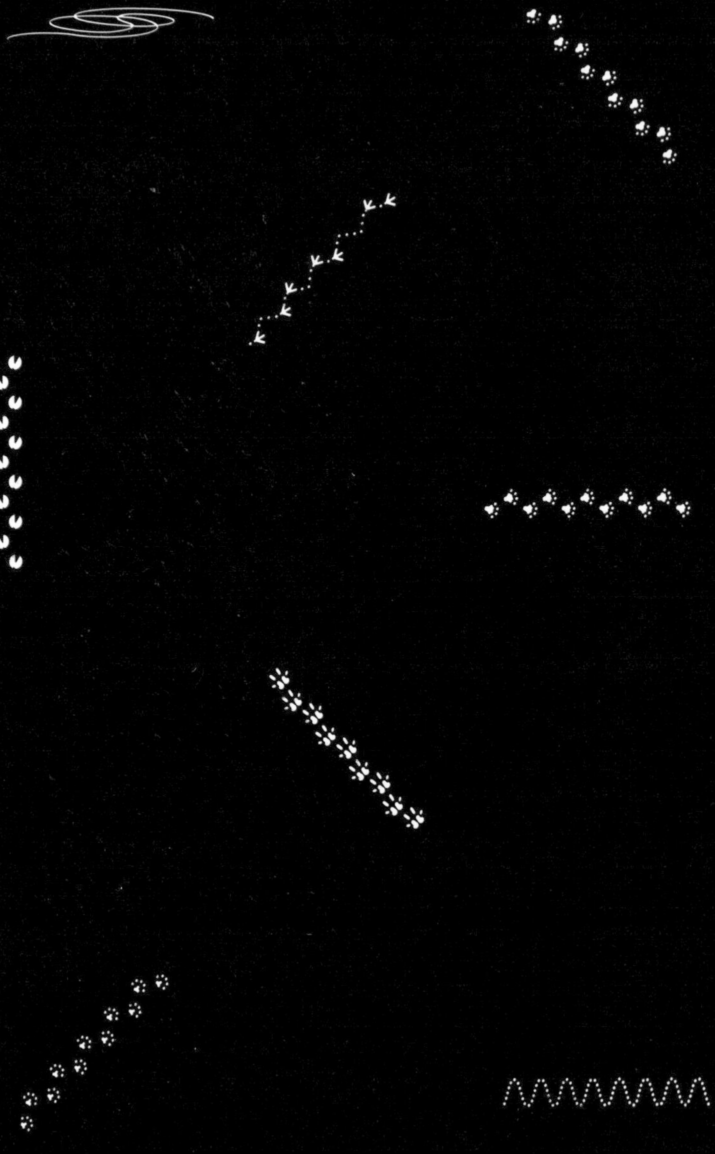